CU00920926

Susie Howe's compelling story reminds
necessary we might just end up doing t
open and honest and, despite the weigl
author maintains a light touch through
as both gauntlet and encouragement to people wondering whether
God is real, and whether they can make a difference in this life. It
may even galvanize a few more dormant 'resistance fighters' into
taking up the fight.
Rhidian Brook, writer and broadcaster

Susie Howe's book is an inspirational read. The words 'If you do
what's possible then God will do what's impossible' come to mind,
as Susie and her husband follow God's call in Africa. Her strategy of
empowering whole communities to look after their own destitute
children is so simple and yet so effective.
Sarah de Carvalho, Founder and Chief Executive of Happy Child

A brilliant, moving, deeply personal, inspiring, faith-filled and
passionate journey about how to change the lives of some of the
poorest and most marginalized in our world today. This book will
make you smile, may move you to tears, will warm your heart and
will stir you to action.
Dr Patrick Dixon, Founder, AIDS Care Education and Training (ACET)

Susie's story is one of courage and a thirst for justice, but above all of
faith. There is such a strong sense that God has had his hand on her
life, leading her through nurse training to the care of people with
HIV and AIDS, and on to an involvement with HIV in Zimbabwe and
then to a ministry caring for children orphaned by AIDS. Knowing
Susie, none of this is an exaggeration, and her heart for justice and
compassion, surely God's biggest gift to her, shines through. A book
to challenge complacency, give hope to the faint-hearted and inspire
those longing to make a difference for God in the world.
*Steve Fouch, Head of Allied Professions Ministries, Christian Medical
Fellowship*

Resistance Fighter is a stirring, gripping, challenging account, which
both warms your heart and makes you want to weep. But beyond
that, it is a rallying cry to embrace costly obedience and gritty
discipleship in our respective journeys. Susie Howe's life is a
testimony to God's power and faithfulness in laying hold of a

surrendered life. She has shown how it is indeed in the darkest places that the light shines brightest, and the work of The Bethany Children's Trust is a beacon of hope to many of Africa's last, lost and least. So if you read it, may you, like me, be disturbed and moved beyond my questionings of 'What are you going to do about it, God?' to hearing his question: 'No, what are *you* going to do about it?'
Simon Guillebaud, Founder of Great Lakes Outreach

The book may be entitled *Resistance Fighter*, but you will find Susie's blend of realism and winsomeness hard to resist. To turn the pages of this book is to feel the hot African sun on your back and to hear the shrill sound of children's voices in the background. As Susie unfurls the story of her work among some of the world's poorest children, it is hard not to be moved. If you are looking for a brash and triumphant tale of revolution, though, this is not the book for you. Susie's tale is told with a rare blend of searing passion and realistic humility. Read it if you dare.
Richard Littledale, author, broadcaster and leader of Teddington Baptist Church

Resistance Fighter tells the inspiring and powerful story of what it means to be an active Christian serving people in the world today, and it awakens us to the terrible reality of life for so many children in Africa. Susie Howe knows what it means to really listen to God and to follow his calling for her life, whatever the cost. It is a fascinating read for anyone interested in working in Africa or with suffering children across the world.
Julia Ogilvy, author of Turning Points *and Chair of Project Scotland*

Resistance Fighter was like a warm, rich, hearty bowl of soup for my soul. More than just an adventure tale, a trumpet is blown for readers to peer in on the personal experiences, thoughts and emotions of Susie Howe's journey in and around the African heartlands. This book is a stirring celebration of faith in action. In the face of tragedy, there is triumph; in the face of despair, there is hope! Confronting the brutal reality of AIDS, poverty and war, each chapter helps answer the question everyday people ask: 'So what can we do about it?'
Dr Robi Sonderegger, clinical psychologist, humanitarian activist and Director of Family Challenge Australia

RESISTANCE FIGHTER

Susie Howe

RESISTANCE FIGHTER

God's heart for the broken

ivp

INTER-VARSITY PRESS
Norton Street, Nottingham NG7 3HR, England
Email: ivp@ivpbooks.com
Website: www.ivpbooks.com

First published 2011

British Library Cataloguing-in-Publication Data
A catalogue record for this book is available from the British Library.

ISBN: 978–1–84474–517–3

Typeset in Great Britain by CRB Associates, Potterhanworth, Lincolnshire
Printed and bound in Great Britain by Ashford Colour Press Ltd, Gosport,
Hampshire

*Inter-Varsity Press publishes Christian books that are true to the Bible and that
communicate the gospel, develop discipleship and strengthen the church for its
mission in the world.*

*Inter-Varsity Press is closely linked with the Universities and Colleges Christian
Fellowship, a student movement connecting Christian Unions in universities and
colleges throughout Great Britain, and a member movement of the International
Fellowship of Evangelical Students. Website: www.uccf.org.uk*

For Poogs
Thank you for being my better half

Our Lord, you will always rule,
but nations will vanish
from the earth.
You listen to the longings
of those who suffer.
You offer them hope,
and you pay attention
to their cries for help.
You defend orphans
and everyone else in need,
so that no one on earth
can terrify others again.
(Psalm 10:16–18, cev)

Contents

Acknowledgments

Of all the different aspects of this book, this is possibly the hardest part to write. There are people without whom this story could simply not have been written, and countless others without whom this story would not have been so rich. It's impossible to acknowledge all of them by name, but God knows who they are, and that's what really counts.

I want to thank my colleagues and co-workers, past and present, for journeying with me, and for allowing me to journey with you. Most of the achievements I describe in these pages are down to you.

My grateful thanks to the people and agencies that I have been privileged to network with – I have learned so much from you.

My true mentors have been the members of communities, churches and partner projects in townships, cities and rural villages in Asia and throughout Africa, whom I have had the huge privilege of visiting and working alongside, as together we have sought to bring heaven to earth. Thank you for your courage, compassion, grace, generosity and hospitality, and for showing me what true love and faith look like. I am indebted to you.

I want to thank my friends for being faithful and true, and for sticking with me, even when I have not been 'there' for you because of my lifestyle and commitments. You know who you are, and I thank God for you.

Every family has its oddballs, and I'm definitely the one in mine! My deepest thanks to *all* my precious family for your constant love and support, and for standing with me, even when you are not always sure what it's all about. I wouldn't be where I am today without you.

Thank you to Eleanor Trotter, Senior Commissioning Editor at IVP, for getting me into this and for your invaluable advice. You're great.

Most of all, I want to thank Jeremy, my incredible husband and soulmate, who has stood with me through thick and thin, and constantly released me into all that God has called me to do. You are everything to me, and I could never have done it without you.

And finally . . .

What a God we have! And how fortunate we are to have him, this Father of our Master Jesus! Because Jesus was raised from the dead, we've been given a brand-new life and have everything to live for, including a future in heaven – and the future starts now! . . . You never saw him, yet you love him. You still don't see him, yet you trust him – with laughter and singing. Because you kept on believing, you'll get what you're looking forward to: total salvation.
(1 Peter 1:3, 8–9, *The Message*)

Abbreviations

AADH	Association Africaine des Droits de l'Homme (African Association for the Rights of the Individual)
ACET	Aids Care Education and Training, founded by Dr Patrick Dixon
APRECOM	AIDS Prevention Care Outreach Ministry
BCT	The Bethany Children's Trust, founded by Susie Howe
CAHL	Christian AIDS Helpline
CBFC	Communauté Baptiste du Fleuve Congo (Baptist Community of Congo River)
CRARN	Child Rights and Rehabilitation Network
DRC	Democratic Republic of Congo (formerly known as Congo and then Zaire)
EPED	Equipe Pastorale auprès des Enfants en Détresse (Pastoral Team for Children in Distress)
FACT	Family AIDS Care Trust
ICD	International Cooperation for Development
IDP	Internally Displaced People's Camps
LRA	Lord's Resistance Army
PCM	Pukusu Children's Ministries

RILPES	Réseau des Intervenants pour la Lutte contre les Phénomènes Enfants dits Sorciers (The Network for Those Fighting the Phenomenon of So-called 'Child Witches')
SGM	Scripture Gift Mission (later to be called SGM Lifewords)
SSN	Stepping Stones Nigeria
TBP	The Bethany Project, founded by Susie Howe
UNICEF	United Nations Children's (Emergency) Fund
VINODI	Vie Nouvelle et Développement Intégral (New Life and Integral Development)
VSO	Voluntary Service Overseas
YWAM	Youth With A Mission
ZBC	Zimbabwe Broadcasting Corporation
ZOE	Zimbabwe Orphans through Extended Hands

Foreword

Someone described Susie Howe as Britain's answer to Mother Teresa. You should read this book and make your own judgment.

What Susie embodies, and her story so eloquently conveys, is nothing less than God's boundless passion for the lost, the needy and the broken. In meeting Susie, you will find, thinly veiled behind her, a God tirelessly working to reach out to his beautiful creation: a creation made in his very image, to be creative, fun-loving, fearless, free, powerful beings in charge of their surroundings and in love with their community, and yet a creation sadly steeped in strife, overcome by trouble and broken by grief.

It should not be so, and Susie has joined God in his mission to make a difference.

Joining God in anything can be somewhat daunting! It is an adventure for sure, but one that will change you, just as it has changed Susie. It is said that you become like the people you hang out with, and if we join God on a journey, we will tend to spend a lot of time with him. The side effect of that is change: fundamental alteration of an otherwise predictable pattern of fearful, self-centred and somewhat pointless existence to one that is extraordinary. What is so compelling about this story is that it reminds us of what an awesome God can do with fairly ordinary people – if we allow him, if we say 'Yes' and, like Susie, join him on the journey.

In days of old, that sort of thing was called 'pilgrimage'; these days, one can pay much money or read weighty volumes in order to find 'wisdom', but the trick is to realize that life is found when it is given away to others, just as Jesus showed us on the cross.

Reading this book will encourage you, overwhelm you and, hopefully, spur you on to follow Jesus in reaching a broken world, to lay aside other crowding agendas and find healing for yourself and others, as you journey in the extraordinary company of saints.

Go well.

J. Patrick C. McDonald
Chief Executive of Viva Network and Senior Associate for Children of the Lausanne Movement

Introduction

I resisted writing this book for a very long time. Many people in the past few years have said, 'You should write a book about your life and experiences', but I have always thought that writing such a book would be self-indulgent, and anyway, I never had the time. To be honest, I have always felt that there are many people 'out there' whose lives are far worthier of being written about than mine.

However, last year I was visiting Dr Patrick Dixon and his lovely wife, Sheila. Among many other things, Patrick is an author, a business consultant, founder of the international AIDS agency, ACET, and Chairman of the ACET International Alliance. He is also an ex-colleague and a friend. During our time together, Patrick kept on insisting that I should write a book. As I left Patrick and Sheila's house and warm hospitality, I knew that the time had come for me to take seriously what Patrick and many others had been saying, so I prayed about it. 'If you want me to write a book, then please confirm it in a way that is undeniably from you,' I said to God. I then went on a working visit to Zambia for a couple of weeks. On my return, I opened up my emails and couldn't believe my eyes! Sitting there was a request from Eleanor Trotter, Senior Commissioning Editor at Inter-Varsity Press, asking if I would consider writing an autobiography. I realized there and then that there was no wriggling out of it! This book is the result of what I took to be plain-as-daylight confirmation from God and my subsequent meeting with Eleanor.

Fortunately, over the years, I have been an inveterate writer of letters, diaries and reports. These have been an invaluable source of reference in the writing of this book, enabling me accurately to recall conversations and situations, and aiding authenticity. Where necessary, I have changed names to protect the identities of individuals.

Strictly speaking, this isn't a classic or complete autobiography. For one thing, it's difficult to condense a lifetime into thirteen chapters, and, in telling my story, I have omitted much that is of a personal nature to my family and me. I have chosen instead to focus on my work amongst those who are treated as social outcasts: the poor and the vulnerable, who, despite their adversity, have also been my mentors. It is they who have taught me what it means to be truly loving, hospitable, humble, courageous, compassionate and caring – in short, how to be truly human. This is a story populated by some of the planet's greatest unsung heroes: co-workers and spiritual kinsmen and women who withhold nothing of themselves to bring about healing and restoration to those who suffer, and whose lives bear authentic witness to the Christ-life within them.

Finally, this is the story of what can happen when an ordinary woman opens her heart and life to an extraordinary God, and tries to live in intimacy with him and in simple obedience to his will. It's part of the over-arching story of a God who refuses to be put into a 'religious' box, who manifests himself in everyday life in a myriad ways, and who stops at nothing to bring about his justice, rule and reign in and through the lives of those who open their hearts to him.

Susie Howe
September 2010

1. 'What are *you* going to do about it?'

'There's a woman dying nearby. Please would you come with me to pray for her?' the pastor asked.

How could I refuse? We walked along sandy tracks, the heat of the sun searing my head. I had left my sunglasses behind, and everything seemed bleached of colour. We arrived at a round, thatched hut, and I paused before entering. I had never been inside an African hut before, and I felt hugely privileged to be doing so now. I was totally disorientated by the darkness of the interior in comparison with the exaggerated brightness of the day outside. For a while I stood motionless and blinking, trying to get my bearings. Finally, I made out a form, lying on the ground to the left of me. This was the woman we had come to pray for. She was lying with her face turned towards the wall of the hut.

I knelt down beside her and gently touched her on the shoulder. The pastor introduced me and explained why we had come. She barely responded. As my eyes adjusted to the light, I gradually became aware that the poor woman was lying directly on the mud floor, in her own excrement. I was mortified. 'Right now, this dear lady needs a wash more than prayer,' I exclaimed. 'Please fetch me a bowl of water, and I will help to clean her.' The pastor and one of the woman's family members lowered their eyes and looked embarrassed. 'There is no water,' they said, shrugging their shoulders. 'There's a severe drought. Normally we get water from the river ten miles away. But the river has dried up.'

I felt a strange singing in my ears, and the world seemed to somersault. The polarity of my life in the UK and life here in Zimbabwe hit me with powerful force. 'Then please fetch me some toilet paper,' I said, somewhat naively. 'What is toilet paper?' was the reply. A pressure was rising in my chest. I had never felt so impotent. Bizarrely, a picture crossed my mind of the comfortable pink-and-grey padded chairs in the HIV unit I worked in at Charing Cross Hospital in London, and of the tins of Quality Street sweets on the waiting room tables.

Somebody brought some rags. 'I'm going to roll you over and make you more comfortable,' I whispered to the inert woman. Holding her frail body in my arms, I gently turned her towards me. At that moment, I was shocked rigid. Only years of nursing experience prevented me from crying out loud. Gazing at the woman, I saw that the entire right side of her face was missing . . . her eye, cheek and lips eaten away by what appeared to be untreated herpes, an infection common in those with compromised immune systems such as those with HIV. At the clinic at Charing Cross Hospital, we simply put patients on a course of Aciclovir tablets at the first sign of a blister, and the problem would normally be resolved. Now, here was this precious woman, dying on the floor, without so much as a paracetomol.

The pressure in my chest exploded. All the anger against the injustice I had seen in the past few weeks suddenly erupted. I was furious at God. I remained silent, but as I held the woman in my arms, I shouted out to him in my heart, 'God, this is obscene! What are you going to do about it?' It was then that I heard his voice, soft and gentle, inside of me.

'No,' he responded. 'The question is, Susie, what are *you* going to do about it?'

That was it. Everything went into free fall in that moment. Life would never be the same again.

2. Childhood

My entry into the world had been unpromising, to say the least. My twin sister and I were born at home in Tottenham, London. After a tough labour, Jane was born first, weighing just five pounds. My poor mother, Pamela, had no idea that she was carrying twins, so when she started contractions again a few minutes after Jane's arrival, she thought that I was the afterbirth! She was horrified when my head crowned, and I slithered out with ease. An emergency call was made to my grandmother to go and buy more nappies and baby clothes. A photo soon afterwards shows my mum lying in bed, cradling Jane and me in her arms, looking gaunt and bewildered. The photo appeared in a national newspaper, because my father, Tommy, was a professional footballer with Tottenham Hotspur Football Club. Jane and I were born in the top flat of a house overlooking White Hart Lane football ground, and Dad taught us to kick a football around almost before we could walk! Footballers at that time were poorly paid, and my mum struggled to dry our nappies over a smoky coal fire in our tiny living room, the sole source of heat in the flat.

Mum would parade us along the streets in our double-hooded Silver Cross pram, with our brother Nicky walking along beside us. As a four-year-old boy, it can't have been easy for him to adapt to the arrival of twin sisters, especially as Jane and I grew up to be exceptionally close. For the first few years of our lives, we spoke nothing but a gobbledegook 'twin' language, and would play happily for hours, communicating with each other in our exclusive language that no-one else understood. But fortunately we began to communicate 'normally' in time for our entry into primary school. Throughout school, we were placed in the same class, often sharing desks next to each other. Until our teens, we were dressed identically, which occasionally caused confusion because we looked so alike. Our personalities were very different, however. Jane was quiet and shy, whereas I was a noisy tomboy, preferring to play with boys rather than girls. I liked nothing better than a dare, and would climb the tallest trees, dive off the highest diving boards and climb over walls to 'scrump' for apples from the neighbours' gardens, in an effort to show that I was every bit as good as the boys. All I wanted was to be allowed to play with Nicky and his friends, and I didn't even mind being the one who was endlessly chased and shot in games of cowboys and Indians or cops and robbers.

My father's football career came to a sudden end with a tragic football accident in which his kneecap was badly damaged. He struggled to adapt to a 'normal' way of life, and eventually went into trade as a plumber and heating engineer. The family then moved to Broadstairs in Kent, and my mum became pregnant with my brother, Paul. Jane and I loved him like two little mothers from the day he was born, and slavishly helped to change his nappies and feed him.

Our new black-and-white television marked key world events, relaying them to our living room. I remember the shocked reaction of my parents to the news of John F. Kennedy's death not long after my sixth birthday in 1963. In April 1968, when Martin Luther King Jnr died, it was I who was shocked, as he had been one of my heroes.

I had a strange ambition as a child. When asked what I wanted to be when I grew up, I would say, 'a resistance fighter'. My granddad had told me stories of occupied France during the Second World War in which underground fighters would doggedly resist the enemy. This captured my imagination. I thrilled at the thought of fighting for a just cause. When Nicky, provoked or in vindictive mood, would give me 'Chinese burns' on my wrist, I would shout, 'You'll never make me cry! Resistance fighters never give in!' My bravado, however, would instantly dissolve whenever I watched *Doctor Who* on television. At the first sign of a dalek or cyberman, Jane and I would hide behind the settee in fear, with cushions covering our eyes!

Even as a child, I was drawn to those who didn't 'fit in' and those on the margins. My best friend, Mandy, lived in a local children's home, and she rarely, if ever, saw her mum. Sometimes, after school, I went to the home for tea with her, where we would eat fish fingers and chips swimming in tomato sauce, and I would play on the swings with the other resident children. When it came to bedtime, all the children had to line up to brush their teeth and put themselves to bed, in a regimented fashion. Mandy often played up at school, but I would try to come to her defence, because I knew it was partly because she didn't have a mum and dad to care for her.

When I was eight years old, a young Indian girl called Mia joined our class mid-term. She was the only non-white child in our school, and others in the class picked on her because of her colour and the way she talked. I befriended Mia, and announced to the class that I would hit anyone who so much as laid a finger on her or called her names. I loved going to her home to play. There I saw a glimpse of another culture, which excited my interest.

I had an innate love for black people, whatever their ethnic origin. There was only one black man in Broadstairs, a Jamaican who worked at the garage on the Broadway as a petrol pump attendant. I would go and chat with him for the sheer pleasure of it. When we were older, my dad would drive us up to London to visit my Aunty Jackie and Uncle Johnny in Knightsbridge. Whereas Harrods enthralled everyone else, I was happiest when we drove through Deptford, where I would see people of other races, wearing different styles of dress.

A map of the continent of Africa had a strange effect on me. I felt restless and sensed a desire for something more than I enjoyed in my day-to-day life in Broadstairs. I wanted to learn about other cultures and to experience them for myself, which was strange, because my parents were far from being the adventurous sort and, in any event, could not afford holidays abroad.

Jane was extremely bright and was frequently top of the class. I loved reading and writing, but was too easily distracted to concentrate on my lessons, and lagged behind her in my grades. I loved trees, flowers, birds, butterflies and animals, and devoured books about them. One enterprising teacher promised that I could be the monitor of the classroom's nature table if I tried harder at maths, which marginally helped to boost my test results.

Autumn was one of my favourite seasons, and I would thrill at the scarlet of rosehips and the deep mahogany shine of conkers. I collected bird feathers, shells, berries and acorns, and, if I came across a dead bird or mouse, I would put it in a shoe box lined with cotton wool, and bury it with ceremony in the back garden, even creating a little wooden cross before which I would kneel and pray for the demised creature.

Praying came easily to me. As a child, I had an innate spirituality and would happily 'chat' with God about things. When we first arrived in Broadstairs, I remember a man and woman arriving on the doorstep from a local Baptist church.

The outcome was that we started going to Sunday school at Queen's Road Baptist Church the very next week, despite the fact that my parents never went to church. Our first Sunday school teacher was a wonderful, white-haired woman called Miss Jackson, whose chain bracelets jingled and jangled as she sang, 'Away Far Beyond Jordan', while waving her hands with great passion. Every birthday she would hand-paint a card for each child. I grew to love the stories of Jesus and wanted to be good for him. I couldn't bear the way he was unjustly accused and executed. The hymn 'There is a Green Hill Far Away' would reduce me to tears, and I would long to fast-forward to the story of Jesus meeting Mary in the garden after his resurrection.

The first day at grammar school was a nasty experience for Jane and me. Older girls taunted us in the playground because of our shiny, brown sandals and because we were 'different'. One of them pushed Jane. Something inside me turned. I couldn't bear to see Jane hurt and fiercely wanted to protect her. I toughened up inwardly and outwardly, and made it clear that we weren't to be messed with. Something of my primary school innocence was lost that day.

By the time we started grammar school, there was one thing that Jane and I both excelled in, and that was ballet. I had reluctantly gone to my first class just one year earlier. Jane had wanted to start ballet, but I was desperate to go to horse riding lessons instead. In my mum's eyes, ballet was more ladylike, which was precisely one of the reasons why I didn't want to go. However, Jane won the day, and we arrived at The Page School of Dance, with me sulkily determined to hate every minute of the class. But by the end of the first hour I was a passionate convert! The tough physicality of ballet came as a surprise, and I thrilled at the passion and emotion of the classical music that accompanied even the barre work. By the end of the first lesson, Jane and I had learned the five basic ballet positions, and how to do *pliés* and *tendus*. Our tutor, Mrs Page, marvelled at how naturally we picked up the movements and, in her words, 'took to ballet like ducks to water'.

From then on, we dedicated increasing hours after school and at weekends to ballet practice. By the end of twelve months, we were featured in the newspapers for setting a national record by both passing all of the first five ballet grades in one year. At the start of the second year, we made the trip with Mrs Page to Freed of London, the renowned suppliers of dancewear in St Martins Lane, to be fitted with our first pointe shoes. I loved the smell and crunch of the resin, as we ground our pointes into trays of it before a class to keep the shoes from sliding from under us, and I adored the sheer joy of being on stage. I now knew what I wanted to do when I left school. Resistance fighter had given way to professional dancer. Pictures of dance legends such as Margot Fonteyn and Rudolph Nureyev plastered my bedroom walls, along with posters of Pan's People from *Top of the Pops*!

I would push my body to its limits and practise obsessively for hours on end. While Jane took naturally to classical ballet, I started to train in contemporary dance styles, particularly the Martha Graham technique that was largely danced barefoot. By the age of thirteen, Jane and I were spending all of our spare time at the dance school, and, when we had performances, we received special permission from our grammar school to skip classes and rehearse instead.

There were several particularly gifted pupils at our dance school at that time, who would go on to the Royal Ballet and other renowned schools of excellence, and we were all extremely close to one another. Unusually, we had a flair for choreography and, for one end-of-year performance, we created a full-length contemporary ballet, entitled *I Am*, to the music of Stravinsky's *The Rite of Spring*. Unbeknown to us, Patricia Hutchinson Mackenzie, Principal of the London Contemporary Dance School, was in the audience. In her words, 'her breath was taken away by the maturity and artistic ability of such young dancers'. She invited us to perform the piece for the principal dancers of the London Contemporary Dance School (LCDS), so that they could learn from us.

It was with huge excitement and trepidation that we headed for Euston, home of the LCDS and the Place Theatre. As the eerie first chords of *The Rite of Spring* echoed around the dance studio, I thought that the dancers who had gathered to watch us would surely hear the loud beating of my heart. At the end I was elated. I knew instinctively that this was where I wanted to train when I was older. The next week before class, Mrs Page took me aside. 'Pat Hutchinson says that there will be a place for you at the London Contemporary Dance School when you are eighteen years old, Susie.' I thought I had died and gone to heaven! Now my future in dance was mapped out!

Although I was a good dancer, I was hopeless at singing. I was therefore bemused when, at dance practice one Saturday afternoon, Mrs Page called me off stage and introduced me to the smartly dressed man with dark hair who had been watching next to her. He turned out to be Tony Hatch, the songwriter and producer. 'I've told Tony about you,' she said, 'and he wants to hear you sing.' 'But I can't sing,' I protested. 'Have a go at singing, "Doe, a Deer",' Tony coaxed. Feeling like a complete idiot, I dutifully went back on stage and gave the song from *The Sound of Music* my best effort, which was poor by anyone's standard. To my amazement, he liked my singing. My astonishment grew when he added, 'I'm organizing a tour of the UK for Petula Clark, and I'd like you to accompany her to sing and dance on her show. Do you play the guitar?' I confessed that I could neither play the guitar nor read music. 'That's not a problem,' he said, energetically.

'I'll bring a guitar over to your house and will give you a couple of months to teach yourself the basic chords.'

He was as good as his word. The next week he appeared on the doorstep, guitar in hand, and overawed my alarmed parents as he sketched out plans for the future. 'Start by rehearsing Melanie's, "Look What They've Done to My Song, Ma". I'll be back to see how you're progressing.' It all felt very surreal. My heart wasn't really in it, as I didn't want to be a singer, but the opportunity to dance on the *Petula Clark Show* was not to be missed. In those days, she had songs in the charts and was well known in the entertainment industry. Every day, I practised the guitar and drove the family mad with endless renditions of the song. I developed a sore throat, and my mum plied me with warm Ribena to try to lubricate it. Melanie I wasn't, but my voice was certainly starting to develop her husky timbre!

But in the end my dad put his foot down. 'You're not going off on tour at your age. I won't allow it.' Back went the guitar, and the house returned to peace and quiet once again.

One warm summer evening about a year later, I was 'home alone'. The rest of the family were at the cricket club dance. I felt tired and was enjoying some time to myself. Jane and I shared a room, and I settled myself on my bed to listen to pop music on the radio. I had just tuned in when I was startled by a clear voice inside my head that said, 'Go to your cupboard. Look under the bottom shelf and fetch the tract that has fallen down at the back.' I sat motionless. Was I going mad? The voice came again, repeating the same instructions. I was just an ordinary fourteen-year-old girl who loved *Jackie* magazine and Tamla Motown music, and who wanted to listen to the radio . . . not the voice of God! But I instinctively knew that this was God speaking to me. I turned off the radio and fervently wished I'd gone to the cricket club dance.

Jane and I each had a cupboard in which we hung our clothes. Opening mine, I knelt down and peered into the space right at the bottom, underneath the last shelf. There at the back was a white piece of paper. I could hardly believe my eyes! With a sinking heart, I realized that this was also where the spiders hung out, and there were a couple of prize specimens guarding their territory. Gingerly, I brushed the cobwebs away and drew out the piece of paper. Returning to my bed, I smoothed it out and recognized it as being something that I had been given a year earlier.

A room in the basement of our church had been converted into a coffee bar for the young people. I had attended an evening event at which a visiting group had played, led by a pretty young woman with long blonde hair and a beautiful singing voice. Afterwards, she had shared her story about how she had come to know and love the Lord Jesus. For some reason that I could not understand, I felt antagonistic towards her, so that, when she came over to talk to me afterwards, I was extremely offhand with her. I remember her parting words, 'It's OK, Susie. You can say what you like. But you can never stop Jesus from loving you.' That hit me with force. I gulped on my can of Coke and moved away from her, but not before she had given me a white leaflet.

I thought I had thrown it away, but here it was in my hand! I must have thrust it into my cupboard and forgotten all about it. Although I went to youth group now and again, it was just for social reasons. The last thing I wanted was 'religion'. I was no longer the little girl who prayed. I'd grown up and moved on from such childish things, and all I wanted to do was dance. I didn't need God.

Now, alone in my bedroom, I read the tract from cover to cover. It spoke about how man had turned his back on God, and how Jesus had come to reconcile us back into a relationship with him. Revelation 3:20 was written out in full: 'Here I am! I stand at the door and knock. If anyone hears my voice and opens the door, I will come in and eat with him and he with me.' As I read those words, they came alive. It was as though they had been written for me alone. I could tangibly *feel* Jesus standing there, asking me to open up my heart and life to him. Young as I was, I knew that I had not only held God at arm's length, but had completely turned my back on him. And now, here he was, pursuing me with his love, inviting me to turn around and get back into a right relationship with him. All my defences collapsed. Suddenly, nothing mattered more. I found myself on my knees, literally crying to God for forgiveness and offering my heart and life to him. People encounter God in many different ways, and some never knowingly do. But that night, I had a powerful experience of him that radically changed my heart and life. As I prayed, I felt an extraordinary 'heat' fill my body and waves of love flow over me. I knew I was in the presence of God, and simply wept at the way I had dismissed him up to that moment. Gradually, a beautiful peace settled in my heart and an almost unbearable joy. I had opened my heart to Christ, and I knew that he had entered my life. It was no longer just I, but he and I together.

The impact was immediate. When the rest of the family arrived home later that night, I went flying into the hallway. 'I've given my life to Jesus,' I said breathlessly. They looked at me as though I was mad, a look that I came to know only too well in the days and weeks that followed, as I shared the news with my schoolmates, neighbours and other family members. Very few people understood. It wasn't just that I now knew *about* Jesus . . . I actually knew him personally. Talking to him in prayer became as natural as breathing. Sensing his presence gave me unbelievable joy and delight. I started hungrily to read my Bible, and what had once been incomprehensible now became clear. I loved to worship God at church and became a keen member of the youth group. I wanted others to experience the joy of knowing Jesus, and would talk about him at every opportunity and join in special outreach events. My family couldn't understand the change, and my Aunty Jean later confided that my mum had once said to her, 'Why can't Susie fall in love with Mick Jagger like normal girls, instead of with Jesus?' Jane was baptized with me later that year, although she would now say that at the time her experience of God was more 'head' than 'heart' knowledge. It wasn't until she was nineteen and at college that she would truly encounter God in a personal way for herself, and her faith would become living and active.

Gradually my priorities changed. Dance was no longer my life . . . Jesus was. I found myself caring about others more. There were a couple of elderly sisters who lived over the road from us called Jessie and Olive, both with degrees of dementia. They seemed to have no family, and no-one ever visited them. They were very close to each other, but their home was extremely dirty and in a terrible, run-down condition. I started to visit them regularly, to help with housework and chat to them over cups of tea. Gradually I visited others too who were either lonely or struggling. My headmistress organized for me to befriend a young girl who had behavioural problems, and my best friend, Bunny, and I helped to bath an old lady at weekends.

'Why can't Susie fall in love with Mick Jagger like normal girls, instead of with Jesus?'

I started missing dance practice. It no longer meant to me what it had done before. I had reached a level of expertise that required hours of practice in order to maintain it. I realized that I needed to make a choice – to continue dancing as before or to give it up. I couldn't just carry it on as a 'hobby'. It was all or nothing. I gave up dancing, much to the disappointment of my tutor, and chose instead to start working in my spare time at a local residential school for children with severe physical and mental disabilities. I loved caring for people, and, by the time I sat my A level examinations, I knew that I wanted to become a nurse once I left school. I applied to St Thomas' Hospital in London, and made the train journey up to Waterloo for my interview when I was seventeen years old. A couple of weeks later, I received a letter offering me a place at the Nightingale School of Nursing, to start in September 1976.

My parents separated the month before I started my training, and so it was that Bryan Stonehouse, the energetic youth leader of my church, drove me up to St Thomas' Hospital with all my bags and boxes, and helped to settle me into Gassiot House, my new home right on the edge of the River Thames. Three other girls shared the flat with me, and, as I looked out of my bedroom window, I gasped with delight. There was Big Ben, exactly opposite. I was back in London and excited by the thought of what lay ahead.

3. A 'Nightingale Nurse'

It was the early shift on the Ophthalmology Ward, and I had been given eight patients to look after. The day was gloriously sunny, and I chatted and joked with the women in the bay as I helped them to wash, changed their dressings and made up their beds. The panoramic view over the River Thames, with its boats and bridges, was spectacular. I'd been nursing for six months and was starting to grow in confidence. St Thomas' was renowned for its high standard of nursing training, and well loved by the local residents of Lambeth. It seems un-believable that in those days we were allowed to wear our blue, striped uniforms and navy blue serge capes outside the hospital, even when we popped down to 'The Cut' market to do a bit of shopping before coming on a shift. The stallholders would call out to one another, "Ere come our girls', and wrap up large packs of cheese and bacon for next to nothing, because they knew that our pay was notoriously poor.

"Ere, 'elp me to get to the bathroom, will you love, so's I can give misself a bit of a wash.' Emma[1] was a warm-hearted, down-to-earth grandmother, with a strong Lambeth accent, and was soon to be discharged home. I settled her on a stool in front of the sink in one of the bathrooms to wash her face, and went back to the bay to make up her bed. Having checked on the other women, I went back to see how Emma was getting on. To my utter horror, I found her lying dead on the bathroom floor with her eyes wide open.

Running to the door, I shouted to the staff nurse who was sitting nearby in the nurse's station. At the same time, I saw one of the senior tutors advancing towards me, with several new nurse candidates in tow. 'This is one of our brand new, state-of-the-art wards,' she was saying, as she got closer and closer, flinging open the doors of the sluice, dressing rooms and laundry cupboards as she went. Her tour of the ward seemed to take in every nook and cranny. I leapt back into the bathroom, closely followed by the staff nurse who quickly summed up the situation. After checking Emma's vital signs, she realized that she had been dead too long to be resuscitated. 'I'm going to have to lock you in,' she whispered urgently. Whirling around, she slammed the door shut, and I heard the lock turn. Sitting gingerly on the edge of the bath, I stared down at poor Emma. The harsh electric light did nothing to soften the impact of the scene. I had never set eyes on a dead person before, and simply could not reconcile the fact that only a short while ago those lovely brown eyes had been so full of life. It hit me forcibly that Emma's spirit was no longer within her. This body lying there was not 'Emma'. It was like a clay model of her. So where was she? Where had the real Emma gone? 'Is she with you, Lord Jesus?' I wondered.

Since coming up to London, I had gone only sporadically to All Souls Church in Oxford Circus and didn't know anyone there. I went home on my rare and precious weekends off, to stay with my mum who was now renting a cottage by herself. Nursing hours were long and hard, and on top of that I had to study. I was exhausted a lot of the time, and had lost a couple of stone in weight in the first three months. The stress of rapidly having to take on extraordinary responsibilities on the wards as an eighteen-year-old was compounded by the break-up of my parents' marriage and its effect on the whole family. I missed my twin, Jane, unbearably at times. She had started at a secretarial college in Bromley, and I saw her only now and again.

It had all come to a head a couple of months previously, when, feeling unable to cope, I had handed in my notice. 'Strong women never give up,' said my mum, when I told her. 'You'll be a disgrace to St Thomas' if you give up,' said my tutor. So I withdrew my resignation and carried on, but .my faith floundered, and I felt very lonely. Now, here was Emma, lying on the floor with her head stuck between the bath and the white pedestal of the basin. All sorts of questions surfaced in my mind as I sat, locked in with her.

Suddenly, the door handle of the bathroom rattled. 'There must be someone in there. We'll carry on this way,' said the nursing tutor. I heaved a sigh of relief. A few minutes later, the staff nurse released me and, after apologizing for the way she had reacted, she took over Emma's care.

Despite this shaky start, I went on from strength to strength and qualified as a state registered 'Nightingale Nurse', as we were known. I was grateful to my mum for not allowing me to give up. During my training, I had experienced the full kaleidoscope of life in all its multi-faceted richness: births and deaths, laughter and sorrow, joy and pain. As is the case for all nurses, my qualification had been hard won, but it was just the beginning.

As a staff nurse, I loved helping to run a ward and mentor the junior nurses, while still providing patient care. Training at St Thomas' was extremely strict, but I believed in nurturing the students with kindness and respect, while still encouraging them to maintain high standards of comportment and care. After a year, I was promoted to senior staff nurse on Adelaide Gynaecology Ward. It was the year that Prince Charles and Princess Diana were to be married, and I was determined that our patients would be able to celebrate when the great day arrived. The nursing staff decorated every inch of the ward with balloons and streamers, and posters of Di in a blue suit, looking out coyly from under a thick fringe of hair, plastered the walls and doors. Adelaide was situated on the eighth floor of the North Wing Block of 'Tommy's', overlooking Westminster Bridge, and I spent hours one day with a group of patients, designing an enormous banner that ran the entire length of one of the bays. With perseverance, we managed to fix it up in the window. On the day of the wedding, as the newly-weds passed over Westminster Bridge, the television broadcast captured Prince Charles raising his arm and pointing out our banner to Diana. It said in huge black letters, 'Good Luck Charles and Di!' We were all over the moon, and fortunately knew nothing of what lay ahead for this ill-fated couple.

It was at this time that a desire grew within me to specialize in the care of those who were dying. Since my experience with Emma, I had cared for many men and women who were at the end of their earthly life. Although I no longer went to church, in my heart I still loved God and continued to pray. My faith enabled me to contemplate death without fear, and to stand with those who were dying. While other nurses would feel uncomfortable around those who did not have long to live, I was happy to sit and hold them by the hand, look them in the eye and accompany them a little on their journey. I found it natural to support bewildered or grieving relatives, and passionately believed in the care of the patient *and* their family.

It was a natural progression, therefore, after a couple of years, to move into district nursing, where I could gain experience in community-based care and practise a more holistic form of nursing. I simply loved it! My 'patch' was a very wide area that covered a large sweep of Kent and some of Surrey. In my blue Mini Metro, I would visit up to fifteen patients a day, run clinics in GP surgeries and visit patients in hospital and hospices. I grew very close to most of my patients. Some were elderly, and I couldn't resist making them a cup of tea or washing their dishes, if they were unable to do so. Others needed palliative care, and then it was a particular privilege to support the whole family through the process of dying, death and bereavement.

Some days called for drastic measures. One morning, there was no answer to the doorbell of an elderly gentleman called William.[2] I felt uneasy and, blithely ignoring Health and Safety regulations, decided to get a ladder and climb up to the first-floor bedroom window of his house. William had been deteriorating, and I feared the worst. His neighbour held the ladder for me while I climbed aloft, trying to keep the skirt of my blue uniform held down with one hand. It was summer, and William's bedroom window was slightly ajar. Looking in, I could see him lying motionless in bed, his face as white as the walls of the room. My heart sank. I opened the window further and with difficulty managed to climb inside and on to the windowsill. As I balanced there precariously, William suddenly turned his head. 'Good morning, nurse. How are you?' he greeted, as though it were the most natural thing in the world to wake up to find a woman climbing in through his bedroom window.

Such were the daily joys and challenges of being a community nurse. One thing was certain – no two days were ever the same, and life was never boring. Unbeknown to me, my career was about to develop in a direction that I could never have dreamed of or predicted. Greater challenges and escapades lay ahead.

4. 'We've never come across a disease like this before'

It was the beginning of the eighties, and I had no inkling at that time of the terrible disease that was to turn the world upside down and cause suffering on an unimaginable scale.

It was Jim[1] who, like dark clouds before a storm, augured what was to come. He had thrown out every nurse who had gone to his house, and had been labelled 'a difficult patient'. 'He's a bed-bound haemophiliac who refuses all care,' said my nursing officer to me one day, 'but we have to try to do something for him. Could you have a go?' The District Nursing Service had a key to his house, and, as I let myself in and walked upstairs, my stomach heaved at the cloying smell of old food and stale urine. Pushing open the bedroom door, I had my first glimpse of Jim, lying naked on his bed as he always did, his joints and limbs grossly swollen and deformed from the multiple bleeds he had suffered. 'Ha,' he spat at me. 'You've come to try and get round me like all the others. Well, you won't succeed. I don't want anyone's help.' 'That's fine,' I replied. 'I haven't come to help you. I just popped by to say hello, and I will pop in again tomorrow.' At that, I left, and returned the next day.

After a couple of days of this, he invited me to make a cup of tea for myself, and, despite the dirty condition and smell of the place, I made tea for the two of us. Gradually he allowed me to change his bed, clean his urinal and wash him. What I discovered was a man who was keenly intelligent but deeply afraid. And what he confided one day amazed me. 'I used to lead a normal life, just like you. As a haemophiliac, I lack an important clotting factor in my blood. By administering the missing factor by injection, I stayed healthy and well, and loved to take a walk every day. Then, one day, I heard that haemophiliacs in America have started dying of an illness that makes them susceptible to many rare diseases. Ultimately they may die blind, demented and without an ounce of flesh on their bodies. I'm afraid that I too will die like that.'

'That's terrible,' I replied, 'but why are *you* so afraid of contracting this illness?' A bitter look passed over his face. 'Because it's passed on in Factor 8, the clotting factor that I have to inject myself with in order not to bleed.'

Finally, I understood why Jim had chosen to live as a recluse and refuse all active treatment for his haemophilia. Despite the agony he endured as a result of the bleeds into his joints and muscles, and despite being bed-bound, he was terrified of a worse fate. 'What's the name of this American disease?' I asked. 'AIDS,' he replied.

I'm ashamed to say that one part of me wondered whether Jim had got his facts straight. How come I had never heard of this disease? Jim had spent days, months and years cooped up alone in this stuffy bedroom, without so much as a window open. Maybe he was paranoid? One thing was certain. He was a frightened man. I wanted to find out more.

It was at that time that something happened that I call a 'God-incidence'. I had started studying for my District Nursing Diploma, and had to go on an intensive three-month course at Chatham College along with a couple of my colleagues. I enjoyed sitting in the back row during my sociology and psychology lectures, with one ear to the lecturer and another to my friends sitting next to me. But my divided concentration backfired on me one day when I missed the announcement that the subjects for our dissertations were being posted up in the tutor's study that lunchtime. By the time I found out about it, all the subjects had been taken by the other students – all except one. Gazing up at the typed sheet of paper on the board, I ran my finger down until I came to the one subject that did not have a name next to it. It comprised just four letters: 'AIDS'. I couldn't believe it! This was the very disease that Jim had talked about. I collared my tutor as she arrived back from her lunch break. 'What do you know about AIDS?' I asked her. Her answer was to become a very familiar one in the next few months. 'Very little, Susie. To be honest, when I first saw it on the subject listings, I thought it meant mobility aids, like walking frames. I believe it's a rare disease caused by a virus. It's going to be a challenge to write a dissertation about it. There's little information available.'

How right she was! It was 1983. Those were pre-internet days, when information was not as readily available as it is now. But I was a woman on a mission. During the next few weeks, I scoured medical journals and met with virologists and specialists in sexual health in London hospitals. Gradually a picture emerged, and it wasn't a pretty one. AIDS was becoming widespread in different nations. Panic was setting in. There were reports that the houses of people suspected of having AIDS were being set on fire. The children of people living with AIDS were being banned from attending schools. But reported cases of AIDS in heterosexual individuals put an end to the myth that AIDS was a 'gay disease'. It was recognized that the virus that caused AIDS could be transmitted via blood transfusions and blood-clotting products like the Factor 8 that my patient, Jim, was so fearful of receiving. I deeply regretted the way I had doubted him.

'We've never come across a disease like this before,' said one professor at St Mary's Hospital in Paddington when I went to meet with him. 'Young, gay men in particular are dying of a cluster of very rare cancers and lung infections. We've no real idea of the different ways the disease is being transmitted, or exactly what's causing it, although doctors at the Institut Pasteur in France report that they have just isolated a new virus, which they suggest might be the cause of AIDS. Patients are being treated in isolation. All of them die in the end.'

What he didn't say was that, because of fears of 'contamination', medical staff were treating patients while dressed in what could only be described as 'spacesuits'. Food was being passed to patients through hatches, and cleaning staff would not go into their rooms. Many staff were refusing to touch patients believed to have AIDS, or to care for them. People were dying like social outcasts, in isolation, without proper medical support or tender loving care. I felt outraged. How could human beings be treated like this?

Something powerful stirred within me, something akin to anger, but much more than that. I can only describe it as a 'roar'. It was a feeling that was to recur frequently in the years ahead. People were being treated unjustly – marginalized and discriminated against. How could I just complete my dissertation and then carry on with life as usual? I had to act. I determined there and then that, one day, I would specialize in caring for those who were dying of AIDS. If others would not touch them, then I would do so, and would give them the dignity and care they deserved. I knew in my heart that that was exactly what Jesus would have done. But how could I break into this field of nursing?

My opportunity came in 1990. Janni was a friend whom I'd known since I was a child. We had gone to the same Sunday school together and were inseparable as teenagers. She was a committed Christian and as mad as a hatter. We would sit cross-legged on her bed, painting our nails different colours and dreaming about what we would be when we left home. As it happened, Janni had also gone into nursing, and by 1990 she had become the sister of the Sexual Health Clinic at Charing Cross Hospital in London. One day she rang me for a chat. 'There's a new position going here in the clinic for an HIV nurse specialist, to help head up the Medical Research Council Concorde Trial. Why don't you apply? I'll recommend you to the nursing officer who will be doing the interviews.'

My heart leapt. This was the chance I had been waiting for! The Concorde Trial was researching the effect of zidovudine, the first drug believed to have an impact on the Human Immunodeficiency Virus (HIV), the virus now known to cause AIDS. The drug trial was being carried out on people who were HIV-positive in several different centres, and hopes were riding high that this was the 'magic bullet' that would put the disease on hold. I was overjoyed when I got the job. On my first day, I turned up to find a waiting room full of men, praying that they would receive the 'wonder drug' that they believed could 'buy' them many more years of life.

I threw myself wholeheartedly into my new role. Our spanking new clinic at Charing Cross Hospital and our sister clinic at The Chelsea and Westminster Hospital were leading the way in the treatment and care of people living with HIV in the UK. They had state-of-the-art facilities run by leading practitioners. I had an enviable budget, and got whatever I asked for in order to help improve the care of our patients, including televisions and VCRs for the ward and waiting rooms, and aromatherapy treatments. Most of those attending the unit were young, gay men, and, in the course of my work, I became very close to them. The clinic was a place where they could be open about the disease that, because of the fear of being stigmatized, they had hidden from others – even their closest family members. Here they would share their most intimate hopes and fears, and I spent endless hours listening to and counselling them, in between taking bloods and monitoring their progress. I loved the work and cared deeply for those attending the clinic. We shared tears and joy together, and I was often invited to shows, supper parties, art galleries and picnics by patients for whom every day of life was something to celebrate.

In all my years of nursing, I had never had to deal with such a complex disease carrying such tragic consequences. Like Daniel,[2] many of those I cared for had AIDS. Before becoming ill, Daniel had been a gifted actor, appearing on many London stages. Now he was skeletal and blind because of the ravages of the disease, and pouring litres of diarrhoea a day. His partner, Peter,[3] also had AIDS, but was heroically trying to care for Daniel with great tenderness and touching commitment. I would visit them at home and listen to classical music with them, while they made plans for a future that would never happen. In the end, I attended both their funerals, along with the entire cast of *Cats*, one of the shows that Daniel had appeared in. I still have the ring that Peter gave to me just before he died, as he thanked me for journeying with him to the end. With every death, I would feel a real sense of grief and sadness, which, far from being discouraging, made me more determined than ever to play my part in combatting this dreadful disease.

Gradually I noticed a change. More and more men and women of African origin were attending the clinic. Some were refugees. I was acutely aware that the information and literature we were offering was geared towards gay men. I also recognized that I had no idea about the cultural and social background of these men and women sitting in front of me, or any understanding of how to speak their heart language. I needed to learn their perspective, but where was I to start?

The answer came as the result of a throwaway remark made by Stuart, a colleague of mine who worked in the Pharmacy Department. It was spring 1992. Stuart and I worked closely together on the Concorde Trial and were snatching a quick break in between patients. I was bemoaning the fact that I couldn't afford to go on holiday. 'Then why don't you apply to the hospital trustees for a research scholarship?' asked Stuart, taking a gulp of coffee. 'It's a great way of getting a few weeks of fully paid travel to anywhere in the world. The scholarships are awarded annually, and any doctor, nurse or pharmacist can apply. All you've got to do is submit a plan for a piece of research that will benefit the hospital, and then carry it out if your application is successful.' 'Is that all?' I replied sarcastically. But that was it. I decided to take a step of faith and apply for the research scholarship. I would apply to research the response of an African nation to HIV.

When I received the application papers, I nearly gave up on the spot. The requirements were rigorous, and I had to give detailed descriptions of the purpose of the research, the activities I would carry out, the costs involved and the expected outcomes. I had drifted spiritually. However, I now found myself praying, 'God, if you're in this, please help me.' As clear as daylight, I heard him reply, 'I *am* in this. Go ahead, and see what I will do.' I felt an excitement in my spirit that hadn't been there for a long time, and a thrill that, despite my neglect of God, he was obviously still very much there for me. But where on earth should I start? I prayed about that too. 'If you're in this, Lord, please give me some kind of direction.' That's when I came across the name of an organization in Zimbabwe: Christian AIDS Helpline (CAHL). The way it jumped out at me was extraordinary. I just *knew* that this was my starting place.

On ringing the telephone number, I managed to speak with Bridget Strong, CAHL's energetic and visionary

Coordinator. At the end of our conversation, she simply said, 'Leave it with me.' Over the next couple of months, she did an incredible job of putting together a proposed itinerary. According to Bridget, I would visit key professionals involved in the field of HIV and AIDS. The schedule included visits to hospitals and people living with HIV in their homes, and doing some teaching along the way. The proposed timing would be January and February 1993. I did the financial sums, wrote a supporting letter and, with a prayer, dropped the application into the hospital postbag.

The call for an interview came a couple of months later. 'We have read your remarkable application,' said one of the hospital's trustees, as I sat nervously in front of him, 'and have decided to award you a scholarship. Are the funds you asked for sufficient?' I could hardly believe my ears! A couple of minutes later, I was dancing down the corridor, punching the air, and thanking God.

I was on my way to Zimbabwe!

5. 'You are a resistance fighter'

Arriving in Zimbabwe was like a homecoming. From the moment my feet touched the tarmac at Harare airport, I felt that this was my natural milieu. It was inexplicable. Bridget Strong and her mum and dad welcomed me like a long-lost family member. Gary, her father, was the pastor of King's Church in Glenara South. His work of reconciliation during and after the War of Independence in Zimbabwe had made him a much-respected Christian leader. Beryl was a motherly, warm-hearted woman, devoted to her Christian faith and to supporting Gary in his ministry.

The first couple of weeks went by in a blur of visits with Bridget to leading doctors, virologists and pathologists in Harare. We then headed out to the eastern border of the country to run a home-based care training workshop for churches in Chisumbanje. Wherever I went, I was seen as 'an AIDS expert' and treated like royalty. But the more I saw, the more I felt as though I knew nothing. A whole new world opened up to me, highlighting the unjust disparities between health and social care in the global south and in the global north. My visits to hospitals in Harare revealed poorly equipped wards, packed with people whose emaciated bodies bore witness to the disease that was ravaging them.

Doctors and nurses were struggling to cope with the increasing numbers of those dying of AIDS, and expressed frustration and anger at the lack of available medicines to ease some of the distressing symptoms that patients were suffering. 'We just have to send them back to their rural homes to die,' said one doctor. 'What we see now is just the tip of the iceberg,' said Dr Timothy Stamps, Minister for Health, when I met him in his book-lined office. 'Who knows where it will end?'

One night after supper, Gary asked me a question right out of the blue. 'What's your relationship with God like, Susie?' I felt as though I had been hit sideways. It was a question I had purposefully avoided during the previous few years, but recently it had crept into my heart again and again. My life was great. And yet, increasingly, I was experiencing a heart hunger for the close relationship with God that I had once enjoyed, before I sidelined him. I poured all this out to Gary, who just smiled gently. 'Why don't you come to church with us tomorrow?' was all he said. So I did. During the service, it was as though every word that was said, every song sung, every prayer prayed was a love letter from God himself. I went straight home after the service, shut my bedroom door and rededicated my life to God. 'I want to come back home to you, Heavenly Father,' I prayed fervently. 'From now on, have all of me.' When I eventually got to my feet, it was as though a weight had rolled off me. God had brought me all the way out to Zimbabwe to get my attention, and now I felt 'whole' again.

The six weeks of my research tour sped by, and, all too soon, I was boarding the plane home to London. 'Fasten your seat belts, please. Cabin crew, get ready for take-off.' The familiar instructions of the pilot catalysed a collective clicking of belts and a general sense of nervous anticipation. Tears streamed down my face. A teenage Shona girl was sitting to my right in the window seat. 'Are you OK?' she asked, with a look of concern on her youthful face. I nodded, blowing my nose with an inadequate tissue. 'I don't want to leave your country,' I wailed. Throughout my visit, I had been humbled by the warmth, generosity, courage and grace of the Zimbabwean people. Their dogged determination and spirit of endurance enabled them to overcome even the most extreme circumstances. I had so much to learn from them. As the plane taxied to the runway, I felt as though I had left part of me behind. 'Lord,' I prayed silently. 'I feel as though I'm going in the wrong direction. Please bring me back to Zimbabwe one day.' It was then that I felt him say, 'Trust me. I *will* bring you back.'

When I landed at Heathrow, there was Jeremy, waiting for me in the arrivals hall. Jeremy was a pharmacist at Charing Cross Hospital, and we had been dating for the past two years. We shared a passion for art, music, ballet and the natural world around us. He possessed a special gentleness, and I had grown to love him deeply. Seeing him made me realize just how much I had changed. How could I possibly convey to him all that I had seen and experienced? Could I even carry on with our relationship? Nothing felt certain any more.

As the plane taxied to the runway, I felt as though I had left part of me behind.

With effort, I tried to get back into the swing of things, and duly wrote up my trip report and gave talks and present-ations about my visit to Zimbabwe at the hospital. For a couple of months I soldiered on, but, again and again, I would think of that dying woman, lying on the floor of her hut in Chisumbanje, with half her face missing. I never saw her again and had no idea what had happened to her. Each time I thought about her, the feeling of anger I had felt as I had held her in my arms would return. One day, it just came to a head. A patient came up to me in the corridor as I was on my way to the clinic. 'Sister Susie,' he said in an indignant tone, hands on hips. 'I *still* haven't had my aromatherapy sessions arranged.' That was it. I felt something snap inside my head. 'You've no idea how lucky you are,' I shouted back, and stormed off. That was when I knew that it was time to leave my job at the hospital.

A month later I handed in my notice, and two months later I started a new job as an HIV nurse specialist with AIDS Care Education and Training (ACET), a Christian organization offering community-based care to people with AIDS. Patrick Dixon, the visionary Chief Executive Officer (CEO) at that time, had founded ACET in response to the stigma and discrimination that people living with HIV were experiencing.

It was good to be back working in the community again, and, together with my nursing partner, Steve Fouch, I covered a large area of London and Surrey, giving home-based palliative care to those living and dying with AIDS. I was in my element. Steve was a highly gifted and experienced nurse with a great sense of humour and huge intelligence. With his help, I got to know those whom we were to care for. Some were users of intravenous drugs and had acquired HIV through sharing 'dirty' needles infected with the blood of someone who was HIV-positive. Others were gay men. Many of my patients were of African origin. Some also had partners and children who were HIV-positive, which meant that the entire family needed care and support.

Again and again, my patients would say that the stigma of being HIV-positive was worse than the disease itself. In the UK press, AIDS would hit the headlines with sensational stories. The fear of AIDS caused firemen to ban the kiss of life for a time, and, on one occasion, some holidaymakers cut short their trip on the QE2 liner when it was discovered that one of the other passengers was HIV-positive.

As ACET workers, one of our most important tasks was to educate the church, which, on the whole, was helping to fuel the stigma. Some church leaders neatly divided people living with HIV into two categories: those who were 'guilty', such as intravenous drug users who 'deserved what they got', and those who were 'innocent', such as haemophiliacs. The gay men ACET was caring for definitely fell into the 'guilty' category and were roundly condemned. Occasionally, ACET workers like myself would be criticized for caring for these 'sinners', not realizing that, in their condemnation and hardness of heart, those criticizing them were themselves sinning. Christ's admonishment, 'Do not judge, or you too will be judged' (Matthew 7:1) was conveniently swept under the carpet, as some set themselves up as judge and jury. It was true that some of our clients had acquired HIV as a consequence of moral and lifestyle choices which they had consciously or unconsciously made, that went counter to biblical principles. As an organization, we clearly upheld and promoted sexual abstinence before marriage, and mutual faithfulness between a husband and wife as being not only a blueprint for preventing HIV and other sexually transmitted diseases, but also for being God's best pattern for our lives and healthy relationships. However, we also recognized the reality that many people were not yet in a place where they could embrace those ideals. For them, life was a messier business and not so clear-cut. Our role was to give them all the information they needed to live healthier lifestyles and to prevent further risk to themselves and to others, and to love and care for them unconditionally.

We were grateful for the many people from local churches who responded with practical compassion and willingly became ACET volunteers, going into the homes of those we were supporting to do the hoovering, washing and shopping, or just to sit and share a cup of tea and a friendly chat. These were the ones who truly demonstrated unconditional love, and the character and characteristics of Christ.

Not long after I started working for ACET, Jeremy and I became engaged and excitedly started to plan our wedding. The preceding months had been quite a journey for us as a couple. On returning from Zimbabwe, my relationship with Jem had changed. He wasn't a Christian and, much as he tried, he was unable to understand my newly kindled faith. Added to that, I felt unable to really share what had happened to me during my time away. It was just too 'big'. So much had changed in my perspective. Although it tore me in two, I felt that I should take a step back in the relationship, and I tried to communicate this to Jeremy. It was a desperately hard time for both of us.

The following month, Jane, my twin, rang to say that there was going to be a dramatization of the Easter story at her church. Would Jeremy and I like to come along? The drama depicted the last days of Christ before his crucifixion and resurrection. The acting was superb. During the performance, I noticed that Jem kept on trying to get up out of his seat, but seemed unable to do so. Later he confided that the drama had really got to him and made him feel uncomfortable. But every time he tried to rise to leave, he felt as though he was being pressed back down, and physically couldn't move. The last line of the drama really made an impact on him: 'If this is true, what are you going to do about it?'

As we all rose at the end, Jeremy was at last able to get out of his seat! We made our way to the exit, and he accepted a couple of gospel leaflets that someone handed to him. At one o'clock on a Sunday morning a couple of weeks later, Jem climbed into bed, exhausted. He was 'on call' and had been bleeped several times that night. Despite his fatigue, he was unable to sleep. Suddenly, his eyes lit on the gospel leaflets that he had been given, lying where he had thrown them on his bedside table. Jem had no previous experience of going to church and had not read the Bible. But, as he started to read one of the leaflets, his interest was stirred. In his heart and mind he had an overwhelming conviction that what he was reading about Christ was true. The words of the last line of the play came back to him with force: 'If this is true, what are you going to do about it?' That night, alone in his bedroom, Jem's response was to read the prayer on the back of one of the leaflets. He gave his life to Christ.

On the Monday morning, I was opening up the HIV clinic when Debbie, one of the receptionists, walked in, a blue envelope in her hand. 'Guess who dropped this in?' she smiled, as she passed it on to me. I recognized the writing on the front. It was Jem's. My heart gave an involuntary leap. Closing the door, I tore open the envelope. 'I just want you to know that last night I gave my life to Christ,' Jem had written. Stunned, I sat down heavily in a chair by the window and wept tears of joy. God's grace was extraordinary. I knew in my heart that we would be married. And we were, five months later in October 1993, at the Community Church in Putney, which by then we had started to attend together.

Jem started a new job as a pharmacist at the Hospital For Tropical Diseases in London, and we found a flat in Ealing where we could start our married life together. We got on very well with our neighbours and loved living in Ealing, where we could enjoy the jazz festival and the beautiful park. Each Sunday we would attend The Community Church. Jem and I were made very welcome, and we started to attend a home group as well as the Sunday meeting. Bob Cheesman was the leader of the church, and he and his wife, Mary, soon became our valued friends. Jem grew spiritually in leaps and bounds, developing a close relationship with God and voraciously devouring the Bible. The day when he was baptized as a sign of his commitment to follow Christ was a joyful one for both of us. Thoughts of Zimbabwe that had previously preoccupied me receded a little, as we settled into our new life together. I was content to surrender our future into God's hands.

Autumn turned into chilly winter. In the January, I attended a two-day Christian Woman's Conference at Ashburnham with Jane. Initially I felt a little out of place with my black, full-length Doc Martin boots, but the teaching was good, and the conference gave Jane and me some precious time to share a room together as we had always done, and to catch up with each other as we walked around the lovely grounds.

On the second day, Jane wanted to go to a session led by a young woman called Kimberley, who was known to be a gifted communicator. After a time of worship and Bible teaching, Kimberley asked us all to close our eyes. 'I want you to ask God to reveal to you how he sees you, as a woman,' she said. 'In a while, I will ask you to share what has come to you, although you don't have to say anything if you'd rather not.' Feeling slightly foolish, I closed my eyes, and immediately the picture of a male, tawny-coloured lion with an enormous mane filled my vision. It was roaring. 'This is ridiculous,' I thought. 'Where on earth did *that* come from?' I opened my eyes, shook my head and closed them again. This time, a vivid scene filled my vision, like some footage of film. I was dressed like a soldier in full combat gear, running through a field, leading a charge. Bombs were exploding around me, and thick mud was being thrown up on to my face and body. 'Follow me,' I was shouting, urging on those behind, as I ran to the horizon. I quickly opened my eyes. My heart was racing. Was I going mad? I decided there and then that I definitely would *not* be sharing anything with the others. They'd think I was mental. Starting at the opposite side of the circle we were in, some of the women began to share how they thought God saw them. Much of it was very predictable: 'a home maker', 'a mother', 'a worshipper'. No-one mentioned roaring lions.

What wasn't predictable was that, from time to time, Kimberley would stop in front of one of those present, and quietly share something about their lives, something that she could not possibly have known without the Holy Spirit's inspiration. 'You are sick, and are very anxious about it,' she said to one woman. The lady in question broke down, weeping. She had cancer and had postponed her operation in order to attend the conference, where she hoped to receive prayer for healing. Amazed, we all prayed for this woman.

The meeting continued, and Kimberley came over and knelt in front of me. 'Oh no,' I thought to myself. But what she said next astonished me, and still astounds me whenever I remember it today. She took my hand and, in a matter-of-fact voice, said, 'God sees you as a lion. You have the boldness and aggression of a lion, and warrior ability. You are a resistance fighter. I see you dressed in combat gear. You are a soldier. God will place you behind enemy lines. You will go into dark places, into prisons, and set the captives free. God says, "Be bold, and do not be afraid, because I will shield and protect you."'

I could not believe my ears. The magnitude of what I had just heard struck home. God knew my heart. He knew everything about me. It was he who had put those 'pictures' in my mind. I looked back to when I had been a child, and, when asked what I wanted to be when I grew up, I had replied, 'a resistance fighter'. I remembered the powerful feeling that would overwhelm me in the face of injustice. A feeling like a roar that would well up inside, compelling me to act and speak out. I started to weep. Over the years, I had struggled to 'fit in' as a woman. I had fierce dreams and desires in my heart that had nothing to do with home-making. I wanted to fight for justice and to 'lead the charge'. Now I knew that I was no misfit. God had put those desires in my heart. It was OK to be me.

There was more to come. To finish the meeting, we had a time of prayer, at the end of which a middle-aged woman with short, blonde hair and a thick, northern accent spoke up. 'This may sound a bit silly,' she said. 'I hope I've got this right. Oh well – here goes! While we were praying, I felt God say that someone in this room has a special heart for black people. God says to you, "I planted that love in your heart. It's part of my heart, and I'm going to use that love as you go forward into the future."' As she finished speaking, everyone in the room turned and looked at me. 'That's you,' they said. 'I know,' I replied, overwhelmed by all that had taken place.

Now I knew that I was no misfit. God had put those desires in my heart. It was OK to be me.

Spring arrived, and with it an interview with ACET's new CEO, Maurice Adams. 'We've been pleased with the calibre of your work,' he said, 'and would like to offer you a new challenge. How would you like to explore setting up ACET in India? You'd be based here in London, but would help to develop home-based care teams in India. It would of course entail a fair amount of travel.' India! My heart thrilled at the thought! The nation had 1.6 million people living with HIV at the time, up by 60% since 1993.[1] The need for HIV prevention and care in that vast sub-continent was urgent. The number of people who could become infected if the disease took root in the 'mainstream' population was unthinkable. I agreed to talk it over with Jeremy and to pray about it.

Arriving home, I found Jem sprawled on the couch in the lounge, riveted by something he was reading in his trade magazine, *The Pharmaceutical Journal*. This was unusual for Jem, as he hardly ever read it, and I often complained at the paper mountain that was being created, as unread editions piled up in our bedroom. 'What's got your attention?' I laughed, as I made a cup of tea. 'A job advert,' Jem replied. I was surprised. 'But you've only been working in your current job for nine months. Why are you looking for a new one?' Jem put the magazine down. 'That's the point. I'm *not* looking for another job. It's just that something has jumped out from the page at me, and I've got a funny feeling about it. I think I should look into it.' 'OK,' I replied. 'What's the role, and where is it based?' 'The job is with International Cooperation for Development (ICD), and it's to develop the pharmaceutical services in a place called Zvishavane,' he said, pronouncing the name with difficulty. 'Where on earth is that?' I asked. 'Zimbabwe,' was the reply.

Now Jem had my full attention. My mind raced. Hopes and dreams surfaced that I had purposefully suppressed. I knew there and then that I would not be accepting the new role that Maurice had offered me. If there was any chance of us going to Zimbabwe, I wanted to be free to go. I marvelled at God's way of doing things. I had never mentioned my desire to go back to live and work in Zimbabwe to Jeremy, but had simply surrendered my will to God's. 'Is this it, Lord?' I silently whispered in my heart. Outwardly, I should have won a Golden Globe Award for best actress. 'Pray about it for a couple of days, and see how you feel then,' I nonchalantly suggested to Jem, trying to compose my features. He did, and later that week, went ahead and applied for the job description. It turned out that he had none of the requirements for the role. ICD wanted someone with experience of overseas development. Jem had only ever been abroad twice – once on a skiing holiday in Europe as a student, and once to Venice with me. They did not want someone who was married. He definitely didn't tick the box there. All in all, it was crazy even bothering to apply, but Jem was convinced that this was the right course of action.

After a gruelling three days of interviews, he got the job! What more confirmation did we need? We knew now that God had it all in hand. With a sense of trepidation, but also with confidence that we were doing the right thing, we started to make plans to leave the UK. I didn't have a job to go to in Zimbabwe, and our visa forbade me to have one. I was classed as Jem's 'dependant', and would only be able to do voluntary work. That was fine by me.

The next few months passed by in a whirl. Packing up our home, selling treasured possessions, and saying goodbye to loved ones was not easy. My mum couldn't actually bring herself to say goodbye to me when the time came, and remained in her bedroom. 'Promise you'll come back to me,' pleaded Jane, bravely swallowing back the tears. My brothers, Nicky and Paul, promised to write now and again. Only my beloved grandmother faced the prospect of separation cheerfully. A committed Christian, she had been a precious role model to me all my life, and I adored her. 'Go and serve God, darling,' she said. 'If I don't see you again on earth, I'll see you in heaven.'

The day before our departure was a Sunday, and Bob gathered the church together to pray for us during the service. Gratefully, we listened as one person after another prayed for God to bless and protect us during the next couple of years in Zimbabwe. Suddenly, a young woman spoke up. 'Susie, I believe that God is saying that you will be starting an orphanage,' she said. I looked at her. 'That's strange,' I thought. I had only done a couple of months of paediatric nursing during my training, and didn't even particularly want to work with children. But these words exactly matched the words of a colleague of mine at ACET, spoken a couple of months earlier at my leaving party. The team had laid on a wonderful meal and a rock and roll dance performance. At the end, we had prayed together. 'A picture came to my mind as we were praying, and I'd like to share it with you,' said one of the home care assistants. 'I see you standing, surrounded by African children. They have their arms raised, and they're begging you for help. They look emaciated, and are dirty and ragged. I think God is saying that you will be caring for orphan children.'

'She's got that wrong,' I had thought to myself at the time. But now, here was someone else, saying virtually the same thing. 'It must be a coincidence,' I decided, shrugging it off. But events would soon prove how very wrong I was!

6. 'So you're the AIDS lady!'

Full of expectancy, Jeremy and I arrived at International Cooperation for Development's base in Harare, having been collected from the airport by Clare, the development agency's Country Coordinator. As we climbed out of the four-wheel drive, two other women development workers immediately came up and accosted Clare. 'I've just had my camera stolen,' said one. 'And I've just had my bag and wallet stolen,' complained the other.

'Welcome to Zimbabwe,' responded Clare, looking at Jem and me. 'As white people you'll stick out like sore thumbs and be targets for *totsis* [thieves]. You'll just have to realize that you have more in your backpacks than some people here will ever own in a lifetime.'

With our excitement somewhat deflated by this grim reality, Jem and I heaved our rucksacks into a grubby-looking bedroom with a sagging bed and pale blue walls, our temporary accommodation for the next two weeks. Three months later we were still there. It transpired that the pharmacist whom Jem was to replace had delayed leaving his post, so there was no job for Jem to go to. Every day we made phone calls and tried to get updates as to when we could expect to move down to Zvishavane, situated in the south between Bulawayo and Masvingo. Every day we were told that there was 'no change'.

Jeremy was fortunate in that he was able to travel around the country, visiting hospitals and clinics, and getting a 'feel' for how the health service ran in Zimbabwe. He had meetings to attend and information to read up on. As his 'dependant', I had nothing to do, and after a month of inertia, I thought I would go mad with boredom and frustration. For years I had been used to carrying responsibility. Now it felt as though my world had ground to a halt. I had no idea of what lay ahead, and was powerless to 'make things happen'. Wheels turned slowly, and the red tape that had to be negotiated to achieve anything was enough to tax the patience of Job.

'Teach me to be still, Lord,' I prayed one day, 'and to learn to live in the present. Help me to make the most of this time.' From then on, I found things a lot easier. I made a point of getting to know the other development workers with whom we shared the run-down house in the Harare suburbs. It was fun learning how to make *sadza*, a thick maize porridge that is a staple of the Zimbabwean diet, and how to cook squash and pumpkin leaves. I prepared meals for the development workers, cleaned the kitchen which was Cockroach City, and generally helped out in any way I could. Finding a rusty, old bike without a proper saddle, I pedalled out along the surrounding roads, revelling in the hot sun on my face and the vibrant pinks and mauves of the bougainvilleas growing in riotous proliferation along roadsides and in gardens. God's artistry was extravagantly displayed wherever I looked. Apart from the flora, I had never seen such beautiful birds, and thrilled at their exotic shapes and dazzling plumage.

Twice a week, we had classes in Shona, one of the principal languages spoken in Zimbabwe, and I flung myself into trying to get to grips with its complicated nuances.

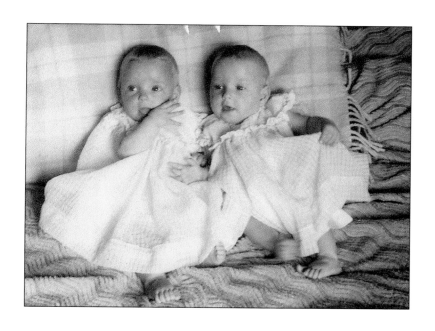

Top: Susie and Jane as babies (or is it Jane and Susie?)
Bottom: Jane and Susie (right), aged three

Susie (left) and Jane, aged thirteen

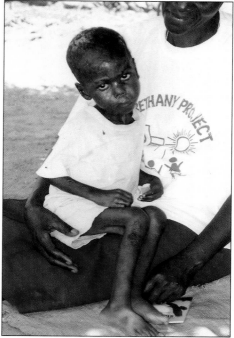

Top: Susie, Senior Staff Nurse at St Thomas' Hospital
(Note the Charles and Diana poster)
Bottom: Taurai with his *vatete*, 1995 (see pages 79–80)

Ambuya Makusha, 1996

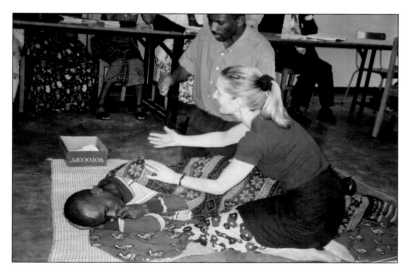

Top: Susie and Jem, 2001
Bottom: Role-play in Rwanda, 2002, as Susie teaches
participants how to care for those with AIDS

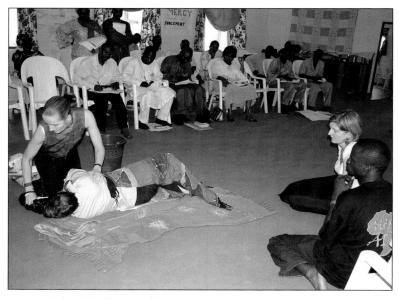

Top: Teaching orphan care to pastors at Iris Ministries in
Mozambique, 2003
Bottom: Role-play in Nigeria, 2004, as Susie teaches how to care
for those with AIDS

Top: Susie with a child from The Bethany Project in Zimbabwe, 2002
Bottom: Teaching little Grace to walk, Zambia, 2006
(Wukwashi Wa Nzambi Project)

Susie with a woman supported by VINODI Project, Togo, 2005

Above all, I spent hours praying and reading my Bible, preparing myself for whatever lay ahead. Looking back now, I realize how important that enforced stillness was, enabling me to shed my old way of life and thinking, and to grow more into my new one. During that time, I learned a deeper surrender to God and a slower rhythm of life. 'Let go and let God' was not an easy lesson to learn for one who was so used to being in charge and in control, but Proverbs 3:5–6 became a touchstone Bible passage:

> Trust in the LORD with all your heart
>> and lean not on your own understanding;
> in all your ways acknowledge him,
>> and he will make your paths straight.

One day, after a couple of months in 'Zim', we went to an ICD conference in Mutare, a city in Manicaland. I gladly accompanied Jem and the ICD team as they headed towards the smoky blue, undulating mountains to the east of the country. Dry, straw-coloured plains dotted with extraordinary, weather-sculpted granite-rock shapes gradually gave way to fields of rich red soil and emerald green tea and sugar plantations. This was the route that Bridget and I had taken to Chisumbanje on that highly significant trip two years previously, and I felt a stirring in my spirit. I suddenly remembered that Mutare was where Bridget and I had stopped overnight with Dr Geoff Foster and his lovely wife, Libby. Geoff was a consultant paediatrician at Mutare Hospital, and Founding Director of Family AIDS Care Trust (FACT), an extraordinary Christian organization that was leading the way in home-based care for people living with HIV. A man of great faith and deep compassion, Geoff was English and had trained with Dr Patrick Dixon, my former CEO.

I decided to pay Geoff a visit. FACT was a byword here, so I had no difficulty in tracking him down. Cadging a lift in the

ICD vehicle, I was dropped off in Mutare, and found his office, which was a bungalow-style house set in a garden. It was good to see him again, this tall, lanky man with boyish good looks, a gentle heart and great humility. At the end of a stimulating couple of hours, during which Geoff talked about the work of FACT, and the relentless advance of AIDS in Zimbabwe, we sat and prayed together. 'You know what I think you should do when you get to Zvishavane?' said Geoff, as I rose to say goodbye. 'Start up an orphan-care programme.' His words nearly lifted me off my feet. There it was again! Orphans. 'Why on earth did you say that?' I asked in amazement. 'Because I think it's true,' smiled Geoff, leading me out of the room. Hiding his words in my heart, I decided to pray about them. 'I've never cared for orphans in my life,' I said to God. 'But I'm all ears. You've got my attention.'

At last the day came when we got the go-ahead to move to Zvishavane. Jem was paid a small monthly allowance as a development worker. We bought a couple of cane chairs and a table, and a few cooking pots and dishes and, piling everything into the ICD pick-up truck, set out on the five-hour journey. Our hopes were high. This was it! As we finally reached the last leg of the journey late in the afternoon, I lapped up the sights, sounds and smells as we entered the Zvishavane District. Settlements of round, thatched huts lined the roadside, and the acrid smell of wood smoke and cow dung filled the air. Goats and chickens foraged in proprietary fashion around neat homesteads bordered by thorn bushes, and everywhere there were women and children carrying pots of water or bundles of firewood on their heads, or preparing meals over outdoor fires. The grey slag heaps of the Shabani mine, and its gaping quarries and sinister-looking mining rigs, dominated the tiny 'town', which in reality was a small growth point. Entering Zvishavane itself was like driving into a time-warp. Dilapidated, colonial-style buildings, with wide, covered verandas and walkways, lined the single, main thoroughfare. The town looked like a somnambulant set from a cowboy movie, and I fully expected to see tumbleweed blowing along the road, and sleepy-eyed residents chewing on cheroots.

The hospital was situated just outside the town, on the crown of the hill leading to Gweru. Driving through the gates, we saw before us a series of white, bungalow-style buildings with corrugated roofs. The pharmacist's house was the only double-storey building, situated to our left, just inside the hospital grounds. This was it! Our new home!

Jumping out of the truck, we let ourselves in with the keys we had been given. Our hearts sank! To describe the place as squalid was an understatement. Random wires hung loose from walls and ceilings, but there was no electricity. Doors and windows teetered, broken on their hinges, and panes of glass were smashed. Everywhere was filthy dirty, and our disappointment was immense. Now I would probably simply shrug, grab a mop and broom and a handyman and determine to make the best of it, but then we were very 'green' and unused to having to adapt.

We sat heavily on the doorstep. 'I'm not living here,' I protested to Clare, who had followed us in her truck. She looked sheepish and acknowledged that she had had no idea of the conditions, although it was her job to have it all checked out. 'You'll have to spend a couple of nights in the local hotel,' she said, 'and then try to find somewhere to live in the morning.' Jem was due to start work the following week, so we *had* to find somewhere to live by then.

Making our way back into the town, we arrived at the Nilton Hotel, right next to the Kentacky Steak House. Exhausted as we were, we couldn't help laughing at the names. Everything would be OK. At least we were no longer in Harare. As we booked into the seedy hotel, it soon became obvious that it doubled up as a brothel, but by this time we were too tired to care. All night the sirens from the mine kept us awake, as did the low roar and rumble of the lorries trundling through the town. Sleepy-eyed, we ate the dry bread and hard-boiled egg for breakfast the next day served to us in the empty 'dining room' by a wrinkled, old man, wearing a faded, red jacket, a dusty, black bow-tie and dirty, white gloves. My heart ached for him. What a life! But at least he had a job.

That day, we visited the mine club and local shops, asking if anyone had a house that we could stay in. No-one did. The heat was overwhelming, and our clothes stuck to us. By late afternoon, there was just one last shop that we hadn't tried, which we discovered was owned by a Greek family. The name of the shop was Acropol, and the owner, Mike Timveous, would soon become a good friend. Big and burly, Mike was nonetheless a gentle giant, with thick, wiry hair tied back in a ponytail. Greedily consuming the ice-cold Cokes that he offered to us, we described our predicament. 'No problem,' he said. 'I have an empty house that you can stay in for a few months. It's just up the road. Let me walk you there.'

We couldn't believe it! The house was vast, with three bedrooms, an enormous kitchen and a dining room, and a lounge that practically filled the entire space downstairs. There were two bathrooms and toilets, a storeroom and an additional outside loo. The garage was large, and it was all surrounded by extensive, unkempt gardens. The whole place needed a thorough clean, but it was in good order. Mike offered a rent that was ridiculously low. 'I know I can trust you,' was all he said.

Thanking God for his extraordinary provision, we moved in next day. Lying in bed that night, I wondered why he had led us to such a vast home. Our few sticks of furniture barely filled one room, and we rattled around in its cavernous spaces with its echoing parquet flooring. We certainly weren't complaining, though, and happily fell asleep, just grateful that we had finally got a home of our own.

The next month passed by in a flurry of activity. I spent most of my time familiarizing myself with Zvishavane and supporting Jem in his new post. The latter had got off to an unpromising start. Mid-morning on his first day at the hospital, the police arrived to arrest one of his two pharmacy assistants for stealing drugs. That was the last Jem saw of his assistant. Nonetheless, Jem persevered and gradually settled into his new role. I continued to try to teach myself Shona, and to get to know the local people. It seemed that everyone knew our business, and talk of the 'new pharmacist and his wife' had spread around town. There were very few white people in Zvishavane, and those who existed lived cloistered lives that revolved around the Mine Club and its bar. One day, Jem and I received an invitation out of the blue to attend a *braii* at the home of one of the white couples. It was a disastrous evening. Those present did nothing but berate 'the blacks'. I knew I had to make a rapid exit when one drunken man started to refer to black people as *munts*, an offensive term for a black, African person. I was sickened. That was the last time we were invited to the homes of the mining fraternity, which was something of a personal relief.

We joined Noelvale New Covenant Church, which enabled us to become members of a ready-made extended 'family'. Piet Erasmus was the church leader, and he, his wife Lorraine and daughters, Vonnie and Crystal, made us warmly welcome. An Afrikaner, Piet had made his home in Zvishavane many years previously. He loved the local Shona people, many of whom were his friends and church members. Very soon we were leading Bible studies in our home and helping to lead worship at the church, which met in an old Dutch-style white building.

Once a week, an older woman from the church called Daisy would come to hand-wash our laundry with a huge bar of blue soap, and then iron it. In truth, I was more than able to do my own washing, but Daisy needed all the work she could get to help her to support her family. One day, I asked Daisy if I could accompany her on one of her visits to a place called Calison, on the outskirts of Zvishavane. Calison was a settlement of destitute people that had grown over a period of time at the back of the mine. As is the case with 'informal' settlements the world over, Calison didn't officially exist, and therefore had no input or support from the district government offices. If you lived in Calison, you were a 'nobody'. Daisy visited the camp most weeks to share friendship, prayer and the little that she owned with the people who lived there. I wanted to see Calison for myself. The visit proved to be another turning point in my life.

Sweating profusely, Daisy and I toiled up the steep slope leading to the camp. Everywhere I looked, there were 'lean-tos' that looked ready to collapse at any minute, made out of rusting sheets of metal, bent cardboard and old pieces of cloth. There was the familiar smell of wood smoke and old drains, and the intimate hustle and bustle of a community living on top of itself.

'Go-go-goi,' ('May I come in?') called Daisy in the traditional way. 'Pindai,' ('Come in') responded an old man, one of Calison's community leaders. After being given his blessing to walk around freely, Daisy led me from one home to another, introducing me to the people who had come to know and trust her.

This was to be the first of many visits to Calison, but the one that made the greatest impression on me. I was shocked by the abject poverty and appalling living conditions. Gaunt, malnourished, elderly individuals and those with physical disability had ended up living on Calison's 'scrap heap'. Notwithstanding the best efforts of the residents, the squalor was profound. However, despite the prevailing conditions, not one person lacked a smile or a greeting, and, when I tried to give some clothes that I had brought to individuals whom I thought would benefit, they led me by the hand to others worse off than themselves. Calison's residents survived as a 'collective', gathering firewood to sell, making brushes out of the tall, surrounding grasses, and sharing what little they had with one another. 'I have so much to learn from these people,' I thought. One of the things that made the biggest impact on me was the vast number of children, dressed in rags, playing in the dirt. It turned out that they were all orphans, being cared for by elderly grandparents. None of them went to school, and they all showed signs of disease and malnourishment.

God was steadily 'undoing' me, breaking my heart for those who break his – the orphans and the outcasts.

On returning home, it was the children that I couldn't get out of my mind. 'What future do they have?' I thought to myself. From then on, whenever I turned on the radio or read the papers, the issue being discussed would be the plight of orphan children in Zimbabwe. Whenever I opened my Bible, passages such as Psalm 82:3–4 would jump out at me, 'Defend the cause of the weak and fatherless; maintain the rights of the poor and oppressed. Rescue the weak and needy; deliver them from the hand of the wicked.' God was steadily 'undoing' me, breaking my heart for those who break his – the orphans and the outcasts. But what could *I* do about their plight?

The answer came over some buckets of fish a couple of weeks later! Popping into Acropol for a loaf of bread, my arm was suddenly grabbed by Mike's aunt, who helped him to run the store. 'Come with me,' she said in her thick accent. 'There is someone you should meet.' Thrusting me in front of an ample Shona woman wearing a green dress and a black wig, she made her introductions: 'Mrs Msindo, this is Mrs Howe.

71

Mrs Howe, this is Mrs Msindo.' Hiding my confusion, I shook her hand across the buckets of fish that stood between us, their pungent smell sealing the moment in my memory. 'Ah!' said Mrs Msindo. 'So you're the AIDS lady!' I eyed her carefully and smiled. 'It depends what you mean by that,' I replied. 'Oh,' she countered, 'word has got around that you're an expert on AIDS. Meet me in my office at ten on Monday morning at the government building. We must talk.' Handing me a small black-and-white card, she simply added in peremptory fashion, 'That's arranged then,' and walked out of the shop. 'District Officer for National Affairs' was written on the card in small type, just beneath her name. 'What on earth was all that about?' I wondered.

Intrigued, I decided to follow up on the hastily made 'appointment', and Monday morning found me standing in front of Mrs Msindo, who sat at her desk in a large bare-looking office. After briefly greeting me, she got straight to the point. 'Thousands are dying of AIDS here in the Zvishavane District, and we need your help.' My heart leapt. What did she want of me? Leaning forward, she continued. 'Because of the numbers of adults who are dying of AIDS, we have 2,000 orphans who have been identified through a recent piece of government research. I want you to help us to set up an orphanage for them.' Her words hit me force-fully, and my body reeled from their impact. An orphanage! I thought back to the words spoken just before I left England for Zimbabwe, 'I think God is saying that you'll be caring for orphans', 'I think you'll be opening an orphanage.' I was speechless.

Mrs Msindo was looking at me, awaiting some kind of response. 'How many orphans did you say you have?' I asked; '2,000,' she replied. 'How many orphans do you envisage caring for in an orphanage?' I continued. 'The government has given us some land just outside the hospital. We could build an orphanage for twenty children.' 'So what will happen to the other 1,980 who need care?' I asked. Mrs Msindo shrugged her shoulders. 'The problem is vast. We can't care for them all.'

I sat there, trying to think straight. 'I can't promise anything,' I finally articulated. 'I will try to help you, but I know that we can't just care for twenty children. I don't think that an orphanage is the answer. There has to be a better way. I will do some research on different models of orphan care, and get back to you.' As I stepped out of the offices into the bright sunshine, I marvelled at the way God had been preparing me for this, speaking by his Holy Spirit through others, through the Bible, and by intimately communicating in my heart. The words of Job 33:14 came to me: 'For God does speak – now one way, now another – though no one perceives it.'

I was excited and full of trepidation. On the one hand, I felt completely inadequate, but, on the other, I knew that this was exactly what I had returned to Zimbabwe for. God had gone ahead of me and led me to this moment. 'I'm in your hands,' I prayed. 'I completely surrender to you and your way of doing things. Please guide me, Lord Jesus, and don't be too subtle in the way you do it. But where do I start?'

Immediately it came to me. Geoff Foster! I would go back and talk with him about the work that FACT was doing with orphans and those living with HIV. A week later, I was making the journey back to Mutare in what Jem and I laughingly called our 'Trundle-mobile'. We had bought a Suzuki Jeep from the proceeds of the sale of our car in the UK. Its top speed was a heady fifty miles per hour when the wind was behind us! The chances of being caught for speeding were slim. Six hours of non-stop travel later, the Trundle-mobile wheezed into Mutare.

After three invaluable days with Geoff and his team, I had drafted a potential outline strategy for supporting orphan children in Zvishavane, based upon the work I had seen

FACT doing. I developed the plan in my head on the long, return journey to Zvishavane. Meeting up again with Mrs Msindo, I sketched it out: 'We'll start with a pilot project in a few of the local villages, where we'll train women and men from local churches and the general community to become volunteer "aunties and uncles" to orphans in their communities. We'll choose volunteers who are motivated by their faith and love for the children, and we'll train them in HIV care, prevention and orphan care. We'll equip them to visit households where there are orphans and other vulnerable children, and get them to use their hands and hearts to give the children holistic care and support. There will be no need for orphanages, because the caring community of surrogate "aunties and uncles" will be on hand to nurture and protect the children and support them in their own homes and villages.'

Mrs Msindo looked dubious. Like a lot of individuals and agencies, her default response to the needs of orphan children was to put them in an orphanage. She knew no other way. 'The approach is working in Mutare,' I enthused. 'It can work here. Remember the African saying, "It takes a village to raise a child." We'll be going back to the traditional ways of *unhu* or *ubuntu* where all are for one and one is for all, and where there is an interconnectedness that means that no man or woman will allow any child around them to be an orphan. It's got to be better than putting a child in an institution. And this way, we'll be able to mobilize care and support for thousands of children – not just the chosen few. Eventually we'll cover the whole district,' I finished, with an expansive gesture.

Mrs Msindo laughed. 'OK, we'll trial it out, but only if you take the lead in it. Nothing like this has ever been done in this district before. For the sake of thousands of children, it has to work.'

7. Miracles of transformation

Standing at the front of the schoolroom, on the first day of our first training workshop, I gazed out over a sea of impassive faces, prematurely lined and aged by hardship. The women wore brightly coloured headscarves and *khangas*, patterned wraps that had been frequently scrubbed by hand in rivers or metal tubs and hung over bushes to dry in the hot sun. The men had donned the best that they could muster: frayed, faded jackets over baggy trousers, tied up in some cases with string, but worn with a dignity and grace that was almost regal. It was August 1995, and the air was still chilly, reflecting the tail end of the Zimbabwean winter, when days were pleasant but nights and early mornings could be bone-achingly cold. The sounds of the chatter and clatter of village life and the pungent smell of smoking fires drifted through the pane-less windows of the classroom that had been loaned to us by the local school.

Since returning from Mutare, all my time and energy had been spent visiting the local district governor, the police, church leaders, hospital doctors and the local and provincial social welfare departments, in order to try to bring them on board right from the start with the vision and purpose of the 'orphan project' which we carried in our hearts, but which, like a baby awaiting birth, had not yet been named. We needed the permission and blessing of the political and traditional leaders of the district to start the work, and their wholehearted collaboration. Crucially, Mrs Msindo had introduced me to Minister Msipa, Member of Parliament for the Zvishavane District, as well as the Chief and headmen of Chenhunguru Ward, the rural area where we had decided to start the programme, because it was close to Zvishavane town and renowned for having many orphans and vulnerable children.

The reception of the traditional leaders had been warm. 'Our villages are becoming desolate,' said the Chief, as I sat with him and his *Sabukus* (headmen), under the spreading branches of a mango tree that had seen many seasons come and go. 'So many are dying of this new disease, taking with them their skills and experience, and the hopes of many. Perhaps God has sent you. I will call my people and tell them that they are to work with you. If you need land, I will grant you land. You have my unconditional support. From now on, you are like my daughter.'

A few local women in Zvishavane had caught the vision and started to work with me, one of them being Heather, a motherly Ndebele woman who had simply appeared at the gate of our home one day. 'I hear you are working with orphans,' she had said. 'God has touched my heart, and I want to work with you.' Now, here we were, ready to train the first group of Chenhunguru villagers in HIV awareness and orphan care.

As I looked around the dilapidated schoolroom, I prayed that God would move the hearts of everyone present. How would they respond to what we had to share? There were so many pressing needs competing for their time and attention. Zimbabwe was experiencing a terrible drought. For the past three years there had been little rain. Cattle were dying. Crops had failed. The cost of basic necessities had hiked exponentially. Politically there was a sense of unrest, as people quietly began to murmur their dissatisfaction with the ruling ZANU–PF Party and the iron-fisted President Robert Mugabe. Life was unrelentingly hard for these long-suffering people. Now, here we were, hoping to inspire them to care for the sick and dying, and for the multitudes of orphans in their communities. Was a return to a Bible-based form of *unhu* too much to expect in these days of severe economic and social stress? We would see.

Gently, Heather and I encouraged the villagers to talk about their lives. Like flowers responding to daylight, they gradually began to open up and share the issues they were struggling with, and their beliefs, thoughts and fears regarding 'slims', the name they had given to HIV disease because of the extreme weight loss it caused. Over the next three days, as we taught and trained them, using the Bible as our 'manual', the villagers became increasingly animated, as they began to see for themselves that they possessed the skills, infrastructure, resources and invaluable life-experience needed to care for the orphans and vulnerable children in their communities. Far from being hopeless and helpless, they came to see what could be achieved if they looked to God for their strength, offering him their hands and hearts to reach out to care for their more vulnerable children. Jeremiah 6:16 became a significant verse:

Stand at the crossroads and look;
    ask for the ancient paths,
ask where the good way is, and walk in it,
    and you will find rest for your souls.

'Our hearts have become hard,' said one older woman, speaking on behalf of the villagers at the end of the workshop. 'We have ignored the plight of our own flesh and blood. We have forgotten the old ways. But now our eyes are open, and we are ready to care for our neighbours' children. With God's help, we will succeed.'

From that point on, our feet didn't touch the ground. Following the approach that I had learned at FACT in Mutare, the communities elected suitable 'childcare volunteers', who then carried out surveys in their villages to identify the most needy orphans and vulnerable children. Calling themselves *vatetes* or *sekurus*,[1] depending on whether they were a woman or a man, each volunteer visited five or more vulnerable families regularly to play and pray with the orphaned children, listen to their needs, and teach them practical skills such as sewing, cooking and cultivation.

Some children had lost both parents, and ruthless relatives had denied them their inheritance rights, stealing from them every last pot, pan and blanket, leaving them destitute. Others were refused entry into schools because they had no birth certificates and were therefore *personae non gratae*. Such children were extremely vulnerable to exploitation and to becoming HIV-positive themselves. It was vital to advocate on behalf of these children who were grieving and aggrieved, to fight for their rights through the legal systems, and to teach them skills that would equip them for life. The *vatetes* and I became familiar faces in the local social welfare offices and judiciary departments, as we represented the children, refusing to give up until we got what we wanted – justice for them.

Many children had to shoulder adult responsibilities, as they nursed one or both parents who were sick or dying, ran their households and farmed their land with very little help. Others had to care for younger siblings. In these situations, the *vatetes* would come alongside them, helping them to nurse the sick, till the land and clean their homesteads, thus enabling them to have time to play and be children again. These *vatetes* took to heart our touchstone scripture from James 1:27 that says, 'Religion that God our Father accepts as pure and faultless is this: to look after orphans and widows in their distress and to keep oneself from being polluted by the world.' Prayer went hand in hand with practical support, and every adult and child was pointed to Jesus, as the *vatetes* shared the good news of a Saviour who offered them fullness of life now, and an eternal inheritance that could not be snatched away by greedy relatives. Most of the *vatetes* were Christians from local churches, whose faith motivated them to get involved. It was wonderful to see the loving relationships that started to develop between them and the children they were helping to support.

One day, I arrived at a homestead to find two somewhat overweight *vatetes* playing running races with several orphans. Despite their size, they were gamely heaving themselves towards a 'finishing line' in flat-footed fashion, their heads thrown back with laughter, while the children sped past them with considerable ease. It was a sight to warm the most hardened heart. A spirit of helplessness gradually gave way to one of hope. 'I have now become somebody,' said one middle-aged *vatete* during a feedback session. 'I never went to school, and I thought I was useless. But now the children are calling me "mother", and my life has purpose.'

> *The* vatetes *shared the good news of a Saviour who offered them fullness of life now, and an eternal inheritance that could not be snatched away by greedy relatives.*

Six-year-old Taurai was one of the first children to be registered with The Bethany Project, the name chosen by the *vatetes* for the nascent programme, because Bethany was the place where Jesus brought Lazarus back to life again. Taurai means 'speak' in Shona, but, on arrival at his homestead, we found this boy lying silent on a rough, grey blanket that had been placed on the dusty ground outside his hut. After greeting his elderly grandmother, Heather and I knelt down beside him with Constance, his *vatete*. Desperately emaciated, his hair had fallen out and his body was covered in sores. Local villagers refused to touch him, fearing that they would 'become infected' with the same illness that had killed his parents two years previously, an illness that was now obviously affecting him.

Gently cradling Taurai in her arms, Constance started to sing to him, and to tell him how special he was. 'We will provide you with milk and peanut butter for you to put into Taurai's porridge,' I promised his granny, 'and Constance is here to support you.' Bit by bit, Taurai became a little stronger with the supplementary food we provided, and the creams we applied to his sores began to improve his skin. Constance visited him daily, strapping him to her back in a *khanga* and carrying him to her work in the field. Over a period of time, he came to know the sound of the jeep and would stagger towards us, arms outstretched. Once in our arms, he would lie very still, a radiant smile on his face as he luxuriated in the warmth and attention lavished upon him. Gradually his granny and neighbours started to cuddle him too, and passers-by would call, *'Taurai wakadii?'* 'How are you, Taurai?'

The winter passed, and the hot, dry season arrived, and with it Christmas. By then, I had developed good relationships with the shopkeepers in Zvishavane who regularly donated food to The Bethany Project, and generously gave soap and Christmas gifts for the families we supported. We selected some sweets for Taurai, knowing that they were his favourites, and, four days before Christmas, we took them to him. For over an hour, he nestled in my arms, sucking on his sweets and pointing in fascination to a fat, hairy caterpillar that held his attention. The next day, he walked out of the family hut and never returned. His granny found him lying dead in the garden.

We wept with her. 'What did we achieve?' I wondered, as we helped to arrange Taurai's funeral, the first of many funerals. The answer was clear. Taurai died knowing that he was deeply loved. Every hug he received had been a redemptive act, healing the stigma and rejection that he had previously suffered. Every cuddle proclaimed the love of his heavenly Father. We celebrated that Taurai had gone from our arms to the arms of Jesus his Saviour. Not only that, but his life and death had changed the attitudes of those who lived around him.

We named the corner of the sandy track where he had lived 'Taurai's Corner', and from then on it became a landmark in Makovere village. Whenever the local people heard the jeep arriving, they would run out of their houses carrying gifts of groundnuts, sweet potatoes or maize cobs as gifts 'for the children'. A fire was lit, which quickly leapt from one village to another. I can only describe it as a move of God. Just as Aslan's return caused Narnia to come back to life, so, by God's Spirit and grace, dying communities started to stir, as hope was restored and love was put into action.

It soon became apparent why Jeremy and I had been given such a palatial home to live in. As The Bethany Project grew, so too did its administration. Our house now easily doubled up as The Bethany Project office and base. Financial grants had to be applied for, and policies and procedures written. Having set up a bank account for the project, accounts needed to be kept in good order, and, once the project was registered as a social welfare organization, the mandatory report-writing kept me typing away until late into the evening. A supervisory board was established, and we received a growing stream of visitors, as people came to see and learn about what we were doing. Chiefs and headmen from far-flung villages in the district started to invite us to teach and train *their* communities.

Grasping every opportunity, we scarcely drew breath: Dadaya, Vukusvo, Ndinaneni. One community after another was trained and mobilized to nurture and protect their vulnerable children, and to care for the sick and dying. Some of those already trained would help us to train others, sharing their experience and encouragement. We organized 'exchange visits', whereby *vatetes* from one village would go and visit those in another, in order to share ideas.

'We've never seen anything like this,' exclaimed Minister Msipa, during one of his frequent visits. He had become a genuine supporter of The Bethany Project, and could be relied upon to put the full weight of his influence and office behind us, tirelessly campaigning on behalf of the children. 'I'm arranging for you to speak on national television and radio,' he announced over the phone one day. 'Everyone needs to be inspired by the change that is taking place here.' He was as good as his word, and I found myself speaking a couple of weeks later on the Zimbabwe Broadcasting Corporation (ZBC) breakfast show, precipitating an over-whelming interest in our work. UNICEF and other key donors began to partner with us, and, from that time onwards, film and radio crews and newspaper journalists would visit The Bethany Project from time to time, to document its work and progress.

'How has this come about?' I asked myself in amazement. I had never done anything like this before in my life, and here I was, leading a budding programme in a completely different culture and language. It could only be God. Most of the time I felt completely inadequate and was constantly dependent on the Holy Spirit for guidance and strategy. Each day, I surrendered everything to Christ, and ensured that as a team we kept our focus well and truly on him. As we did so, miracles of transformation started to happen.

One day, Ambuya (Granny) Makusha called out to me as I passed her hut. *'Amai Nherera.'* This was the name that I had been given by the local people, meaning 'Mother of Orphans'. By then, I could speak basic Shona and knew how to dress and comport myself as a woman according to local customs and culture. I gladly accepted Ambuya's invitation to share a cup of water. The heat of the sun was punishing, and I was weary from having walked for several hours from one village to the next, visiting different families and assessing the progress of the work with some of the *vatetes*.

Ducking my head, I savoured the cool shade of the interior of Ambuya Makusha's terracotta-coloured hut, and sat down next to her on a straw mat. Crinkling up her unusual, amber-coloured eyes, she took hold of my hands. 'I know I am an old woman, and I have no education. As you can see, I am poor and I have little to offer. But I have love in my heart. What can I do to help the children?' 'How can you say that you have little to offer?' I laughed, giving her a big hug. 'Many children have lost their parents, aunties and uncles. Some have lost grandparents. They desperately need you to be their granny. If you are willing, we will find some new grandchildren for you to adopt!'

The opportunity came almost immediately. At one of our monthly village meetings, some *vatetes* reported that a new family had come to their attention. Five orphans had recently moved from another district to live with their aunt and grandmother, not far from where Taurai had lived. 'Their parents died of AIDS,' explained Berita, a round-faced young woman who was The Bethany Project Coordinator for her group of villages. 'The grandmother is demented,' she continued, 'and, because the aunt loves the children, she prostitutes herself to pay for their school fees.' So far, the story was a tragically familiar one. How many times had we heard it, or variations on a similar theme? 'That's not all,' added Berita, referring to her worn notebook to check her facts. 'Etina, the ten-year-old girl, has just been thrown out of school for being "rude". She simply refuses to speak.

No-one can get a sound out of her. Apparently she's been like this for several months.'

We were sitting on the beaten mud floor of the small hut that we used for meetings, and my legs had become numb. 'There must be a good reason for her silence,' I commented, shifting my position. 'There is,' replied Berita. 'When we went to speak to the aunt, she told us that over a period of time, after her parents died, one of Etina's neighbours had repeatedly raped her. He's now in prison. Since then Etina has been mute, and no longer knows how to smile. That's why the children have moved here.' *'Maiwei,'* murmured the *vatetes* in unison, shaking their heads sadly. 'My goodness! What kind of a man does such a thing?'

Again and again, we came across orphans and other vulnerable children who were being preyed upon and raped by men who took advantage of their defenceless situation. A myth was being spread by certain *n'angas* (traditional healers) that men could be cured of AIDS by having sexual intercourse with a virgin girl. Even babies and toddlers were being brutally violated.

With the help of the Social Welfare Department, The Bethany Project launched a Child Protection Campaign in all the villages that we were working in, encouraging zero tolerance towards any kind of child abuse. With the collaboration of traditional leaders, police, the Social Welfare Department and the hospital, we introduced a reporting mechanism and system whereby violated girls or boys could be seen immediately by a female police officer, and taken straight to the hospital, accompanied by a woman whom they trusted. There was an increase in reports of child abuse, with some of the cases successfully going to court.

'What can we do about Etina?' I wondered. There were no trained counsellors available, no child psychologists to refer her to. It was then that Ambuya Makusha came to mind! With the permission of Etina's aunt, grandmother and siblings, we would encourage Ambuya Makusha to befriend them.

Ambuya Makusha and the family hit it off straightaway! Armed with knitting needles and a ball of wool, she started to visit Etina at her homestead twice a week. Sitting with Etina on a mat, she began to teach her how to knit. As she gently helped Etina with her dropped stitches, she would sing songs and tell her Bible stories. But still Etina remained silent.

After a couple of months, Etina started to look out for Makusha from the gate of her homestead, and would silently fling her arms around her when she eventually arrived. One memorable day, Ambuya was knitting and chatting with Etina as usual, when she inadvertently used the wrong word for 'house'. Instantly Etina burst out laughing! 'You used the wrong word,' she giggled, as Ambuya looked at her in astonishment. 'You should have said *"imba"*.' The effect of Etina's trauma was broken! She had started to speak again!

Etina was enrolled back at school, but with a female teacher this time, and The Bethany Project paid for her school fees so that her aunt no longer had to prostitute herself. Through her simple acts of love and kindness, Makusha was instrumental in bringing about a miracle in Etina's life. The scripture in Isaiah 61:1–3 was brought alive as God used ordinary people like Makusha to do extraordinary things:

The Spirit of the Sovereign LORD is on me,
    because the LORD has anointed me
    to preach good news to the poor.
He has sent me to bind up the broken-hearted,
    to proclaim freedom for the captives
    and release from darkness for the prisoners,
to proclaim the year of the LORD's favour
    and the day of vengeance of our God,
to comfort all who mourn,
    and provide for those who grieve in Zion –

to bestow on them a crown of beauty
    instead of ashes,
the oil of gladness
    instead of mourning,
and a garment of praise
    instead of a spirit of despair.

But it wasn't all plain sailing. As the work grew, so too did the pressures on Jeremy and me. Every day, women carrying babies, and men in rags, would come to our gates asking for help, and we would have to try to discern who was genuine and who was not, and how best to help them. Some people concocted fictitious stories in the hope of getting money out of us. A boy whom we had helped later burgled us, and someone we knew well stole goods from our home over a period of time, which hurt a lot, not because of the things that they stole, but because of the breach of trust. We knew, however, that it was all part of the territory in a society where poverty demeans desperate people. All we could do was choose to love and to forgive.

For this reason, we particularly valued the genuine friend-ships that had developed with local people in the Zvishavane community. We became very close to Bharat and Ranjan, Harry and Ranjina, who were Hindu shopkeepers with whom we often shared laughter-filled evenings, eating delicious, home-made curries, and watching vibrant-coloured Bollywood movies on their television – a luxury item in Zvishavane. Dr Shaffik and his wife were a Muslim couple who lived at the hospital, and we loved being in their kind and gentle company, drinking cups of spiced tea laced with cardamom pods.

Sipiwe and Makalisa, from our church, were also particu-larly close to us. They lived in a tiny, sparsely furnished, two-roomed dwelling owned by the mine in Maglas Town-ship. Jem and I often visited them on a Saturday evening, when we would sit on their doorstep drinking Coca Cola, eating rice, and singing songs with them and their three young children, the youngest of whom had the exotic name Mona Lisa. Gazing up at the dense canopy of stars together, we would enjoy the heavy scent of the waxy magnolias, the cool gentleness of the night air and the ease of one another's company. Initially, locals would come by to stare at this strange phenomenon of a white couple sharing a meal and friendship with a black couple, but soon the novelty wore off, and nobody took any notice.

The legacy of colonialism and the conditioning of centuries cast us into certain stereotypes in the minds and eyes of people who didn't know us. Because of our white skin, Jem and I would attract a crowd of people wherever we went. I hated the 'white' label, and at times craved anonymity. Our visits to our friends were all the more precious, because there we were accepted simply as 'Jeremy and Susie'.

Despite the warmth and kindness of our Zimbabwean 'family', I missed my family and friends in the UK terribly, especially my nephews, Jack and Ben, and Bethany, my niece. All of them were under eleven years of age, and it was hard missing their 'milestones' as they grew and developed into energetic children. As representative and Administrator for The Bethany Project in the UK, my twin Jane became a one-woman wonder, tirelessly raising awareness of what the project was doing, and helping me to write and distribute a monthly newsletter to the burgeoning number of supporters.

So I was beside myself with excitement when I learned that Jane was coming out to Zimbabwe to visit us during our second year. Not only did we visit the majestic Victoria Falls and a game park, but Jane was also able to see the work of The Bethany Project first-hand. Inspired, and with her understanding deepened, she was able to communicate to our UK supporters in a fresh, new way.

Their commitment and support were invaluable. Local villagers did their best to provide food and assistance to the vulnerable children in their communities, but, in reality, the need outstripped all locally available resources in such an economically impoverished society. As The Bethany Project grew, so too did the need for external support, as we started to supplement the cost of school fees and medical and nutritional care for hundreds of orphans and vulnerable children. Heather and I spent hours queuing at Zvishavane Post Office to take possession of the countless boxes of clothing, blankets and other material goods that Jane and other stalwart supporters had collected and posted.

There never seemed to be enough hours in the day for Jeremy and me. It wasn't just the work at the hospital and that of The Bethany Project that demanded our time and attention. Jeremy had a gift and a passion for Bible teaching, and most Saturdays and Sunday afternoons we would accompany Pastor Piet to the rural reserves that surrounded Zvishavane, in order to encourage and teach small churches which met in the homes of some of the villagers. We loved driving out along rutted, pot-holed tracks to the rural areas, with their hazy blue hills and rocky outcrops.

After six months of being in Zvishavane, the drought of three years mercifully broke, and the rains transformed the parched, bleached land into a lush and verdant Eden. Dark green fields of swaying maize sprang up, and with them fresh hope. 'It is your coming that has brought the rains,' declared the Chief of Mazhoa as he welcomed us to his village. 'God favours you. Please come and preach in my homestead.' Assuring him that we were just ordinary people, we accepted his invitation, and Jem shared God's Word, accompanied by braying donkeys and the persistent clanking of cowbells, as we sat outside, with chickens scratching in the dust around us. Over time the churches grew, and

Jeremy helped Pastor Piet to disciple those who were coming to faith in Christ. We were never to lose the sense of privilege and honour that God was using us in this way.

However, the relentless pace took its toll. I seemed to have permanent stomach cramps that frequently sent me diving to the nearest fly-infested pit latrine. Jem became prone to chest infections and succumbed to a severe bout of chickenpox. One morning, I awoke to find his side of the bed empty. I was physically exhausted, and happily luxuriated under the canopy of our mosquito net for a few more minutes until a call of nature dragged me reluctantly out of bed. Reaching the toilet, I was horrified to find Jeremy collapsed on the floor in a pool of sweat and vomit. He was cold, clammy and very pale, displaying obvious signs of shock. When I tried to touch him, he literally screamed in pain. The nurse in me kicked in. There were no emergency services, and there was no-one around to help. Praying fervently and with a strength I didn't know I possessed, I somehow managed to dress and carry Jem downstairs and drive him to the hospital. Dr Sharrif ran to the car and took charge. It transpired that Jeremy had kidney stones, and he was admitted to a side ward, where Dr Sharrif cared for him like a son.

Not to be upstaged by Jem, I collapsed the next day in the hospital loo, while visiting him. 'Is this a family booking?' laughed Dr Sharrif, as I was laid on a bed next to Jem. I was diagnosed with a parasitic infection called giardiasis, which was to play havoc with my guts for several years to come. Every member of the hospital staff came to visit us, along with friends from the church and the project. We were over-whelmed with their love, as they brought wild flowers, bits of food and boiled water.

When I had recovered enough to get back out to the villages, one old woman took one look at my diminished frame and gave me a big hug. 'You are now my daughter,' she said in a firm voice, 'and, as a mother, I am going to feed you.' Whenever I passed her way, she would pull me into her hut and sit and watch while I consumed the plate of cooked nhimo beans or mealie cobs that she had placed in front of me, and she would always send me on my way with baskets of sweet potatoes and lengths of sweet sugar cane.

Despite the multiple challenges we faced daily, Jeremy and I had grown to love Zimbabwe and its people with a passion. As the end of his two-year contract with ICD drew nearer, we both knew that there was no way we wanted to return to the UK. There was still so much to do and learn. After praying about it, we were granted a visa and a contract that would enable us to remain in the country for at least another couple of years. We were over the moon.

Little did we know that God had other plans, and that we would be returning to the UK sooner than we had anticipated!

8. 'Bring home Jem and Susie'

'What do you want to be when you grow up?' I asked the roomful of children sitting crossed-legged in front of me. Like a choreographed movement, hands shot up enthusiastically and fingers clicked, as some of the children looked as though they would burst in their effort to attract my attention.

I pointed to Charles, a diminutive ten-year-old with enormous dark eyes and thick, black lashes. His father had died, and his sick and desperate mother had simply walked out of their hut one day, abandoning her five children. Local villagers had found them dressed in filthy rags, their hair long and matted, and eating rats to survive. With the encouragement of the village Chief, neighbours rallied to care for the children. Now Charles's thirteen-year-old sister, Chiedza, was caring for him and his siblings, with support from two project *vatetes*. Standing up, Charles addressed the rest of the children. 'My greatest ambition when I grow up is to live to grow old,' was his poignant response to my question.

The luxury of living into old age was not something that Charles and his friends could take for granted. The potent combination of poverty and AIDS had reduced the average life expectancy of a Zimbabwean to fifty-two years. On average, 600 people a week were dying of AIDS in the nation. It was estimated that, by the new millennium, 45% of Zimbabwe's children would be orphans.

That was why we had started the 'Anti-AIDS Club' that met on a Saturday in the huge downstairs room of our house. It was essential that we tried to prevent this generation of Zvishavane's children from acquiring HIV. Their sick and dying parents had had grannies and granddads to step into the breach and care for them and the children they had left behind. Now, with the death of thousands of parents, who would care for a new generation of orphans? We wanted to see this generation of vulnerable children raised up to fulfil their God-given destinies, and leading the way in shaping their communities and nation, both then and in the future. Helping the children to catch a sense of hope was vital if we were to encourage them to make choices for their lives and relationships that would run counter to some of the values, beliefs and influences that had led to the deaths of their parents. Biblical principles that led to health and wholeness, instead of sickness and death, underpinned all of our teaching.

Bare, except for matting on the floor, the downstairs room of our home was the perfect place to teach the children HIV awareness, prevention and life skills, through games, discussions and fun activities. At the end of the morning, the children would run outside, laughing and chattering, to play ball games in our yard, or to enjoy the fragrant fruit from our mango and guava trees when they were in season. Before each club, I would go through the house and garden with a broom made of reeds, sweeping out scorpions that had a nasty habit of lurking in corners and crevices, and checking for snakes, which made an unwelcome appearance from time to time, although Choux-Choux, our cat, was a legend at catching and killing them.

One Saturday, just before the club was due to start, I found a dying, tawny-coloured feral dog that had crawled into our outside toilet. Fortunately, the vet from Bulawayo was visiting the town that day. I tracked him down, and he agreed to come and assess the dog. 'The kindest thing to do is to put it to sleep,' he pronounced, on seeing its miserable condition. Drawing up an enormous syringe, he handed it over to me. 'You do it,' he said, backing out of the door. 'It might be dangerous, or even have rabies. I don't want to take the risk.' 'Great,' I thought, but, steeling myself, I managed to put the poor creature out of its misery before the children arrived, although it upset me terribly to do so.

Gradually, the *vatete* started to run anti-AIDS clubs in their villages. We initiated similar clubs in primary and secondary schools in the local townships, and trained the teachers to continue to develop and oversee them. The children themselves started to write songs and dramas and organize HIV-awareness events. It was exciting to see them leading the way in opening up dialogues about HIV in their communities, and encouraging their peers and parents to choose patterns of behaviour that would reduce the risk of acquiring the disease. 'Our children have become the elders in our villages,' said one chief, 'and we are the ones who are now learning from them.'

It was thrilling to see how attitudes had changed in the two years that Jeremy and I had been living and working in Zvishavane. People were now willing to stand up and talk openly about HIV, instead of alluding to it only in murmurs and metaphors.

The Bethany Project had taken on a life and momentum of its own. A couple of women called Patience and Martha helped Heather and me with the administration and training, while village coordinators monitored the work on the ground. Communities were increasingly finding their own solutions to the challenges their children were facing. Village members repaired the dilapidated homes of vulnerable children, and huts were built for those who were homeless. The *vatetes*, children and whole communities initiated income-generating projects to help towards the children's school and medical fees. Forming themselves into small cooperatives, they made and sold delicious peanut butter and sunflower oil. Others sewed and sold school uniforms. We secured an agreement with a couple of rural schools that parents and caregivers would make bricks to help build new schoolrooms in exchange for free schooling for their children for that year. Even the small white community in Zvishavane was now wholeheartedly giving its support to the work of The Bethany Project, and the Mine, Rotary and Lions Clubs held regular fundraising events.

By January 1998 the government had finally woken up to the fact that nearly a million of its children were living in crisis. It mandated that every province, district and village should form Child Welfare Forums to promote the care and protection of vulnerable children. The Bethany Project was well ahead of the game, having done exactly that in the twelve wards in which we were working. I received a call from the District Governor. 'We're out of our depth. Please would Bethany Project help us to set up the new Child Welfare Forum?' he pleaded. We were happy to comply. Together with the District Social Welfare Department and other representatives from governmental and non-governmental services, we helped to plan a strategy for greater coordination of existing services and the improved care and protection of children in the district.

Each month saw me criss-crossing Zimbabwe in our bright red project truck, the poor Trundle-mobile having died a death after being driven off-track and across dried-up riverbeds one time too many. Together with The Bethany Project team, I continued to mobilize more and more communities in the 'hearts-and-hands' care of vulnerable children, calling churches and local and national leaders to action on their behalf, and campaigning for their rights.

With each new development, I marvelled at the way God was working through us, and that he was using me, of all people, to help to lead the work forward. There was something almost funny about it. It really was a case of God using 'the foolish things of the world to shame the wise' (1 Corinthians 1:27). I had no degree. Nothing to qualify me in a worldly sense for the work. Just a calling from God, a capacity to care and to love deeply, and a passion for God's kingdom and his justice to become a living reality in Zvishavane. As I trusted God and took him at his word, things happened.

The months rolled by, and, with them, a sense that change was on its way. In May 1996 we had received a letter from Bob, our pastor in Putney, which had given us food for thought. In his black, forward-sloping script he had written, 'A while ago, I was in a meeting. While listening, I received from God what seemed like a definite instruction, "Bring home Jem and Susie for training in church leadership." It was like the corner of a curtain covering the future being lifted. What I saw was Jem being trained to lead the church here in Putney when I leave, while Susie

There was something almost funny about it. It really was a case of God using 'the foolish things of the world to shame the wise'.

was working all over Africa with children in need, but with a base at home. It seems to me that you can stay where you are, affecting just the lives of the children in Zvishavane, or come back home and, through "Bethany", reach many more in many other places.'

The letter unsettled us. We had no desire to leave Zimbabwe, but, on the other hand, we had huge respect for

Bob. As a mature and wise man of God, we knew that he would not have written this lightly, and that he could be trusted totally. We simply replied that we would pray about what he had written, but that we had no sense that it was right to leave Zimbabwe in a hurry.

Jem had completely streamlined and turned around the district pharmaceutical services, saving the hospital over a million Zimbabwean dollars a year (a huge amount of money in those days), and making them more efficient and easier for local people to access and use. Pharmacy clinics had been established in the rural areas, and ICD was using Jem to roll out his approach at a national level. However, over time, Jem started to feel increasingly that being involved in church leadership was something he wanted to explore. Virtually every Saturday and Sunday, he was helping to lead the church at Noelvale and preaching out in the rural churches. He had a gift for Bible teaching and a heart to see people coming into a relationship with Jesus Christ. It was now 1997. Something new had begun to stir in Jem, and he started to talk about us returning home the following year.

Living in Zvishavane was a bit like living in a bubble. In a situation where the challenges of daily life were more extreme, we tended to conserve our energies by focusing on our immediate environment, rather than looking further afield. It didn't help that there was little coverage of international news in the local media, and we had no television. However, from time to time the wider world would break in upon us like a rogue wave on a small island.

The news of Princess Diana's death came in just such a manner during the Sunday service at Noelvale on 31 August 2007, leaving us gasping and shocked. 'We would like to spend a moment in silence for the British people,' Pastor Piet had announced, 'and to extend our condolences to Jeremy and Susie for the loss of their Princess, Diana.' This was the first we had heard of it, and, for some reason, her tragic death affected us profoundly. It seemed to make no sense. Every single day we encountered death in Zvishavane. The death of 'Princess Di' was not more important. It simply gave us a focus for a lot of pent-up grief and made us feel far from home.

The new planting season had arrived. A hired tractor had ploughed the fields of the orphan families, and the maize seed had been sown. Out of the blue one day, I received a telephone call from Bryan Stonehouse, who had been youth leader at my church in Broadstairs all those moons ago. It was he who had helped me to move up to London to start my nursing training, and I had kept in close contact with him and his wife, Joyce, ever since. He was working with Scripture Gift Mission (SGM) in London and regularly received our Bethany Project newsletter. 'I'll be passing through Zimbabwe in November on my way to an SGM conference in South Africa. Can I come and stay overnight with you?' he asked over the crackling line, like a voice from another planet. I was thrilled to hear from Bryan, but had no idea just how significant his visit would turn out to be.

Upon his arrival, Bryan pulled out from his bag scented toiletries, marmalade, Marmite and chocolate, like a veritable magician! We were ecstatic! Having had a very predictable and fairly basic diet for the past two years and nine months, these were welcome treats that we wanted to share with our friends. The next twenty-four hours were mad, as I took Bryan around Zvishavane and out to Siboza, one of the rural reserves, to visit some of the families. I was already familiar with the organization Bryan worked for. The Bethany Project was using some of SGM's little Bible booklets that had been translated into Shona, and the *vatetes* would share them with the families we visited. These booklets literally became lifelines to those who read the scripture verses in them over and over again, as they lay on maize sacks on the floor, knowing that their days on earth were numbered.

Gladys was one such woman, whom I visited with Bryan and Gladys's *vatete*. Lying on the floor, covered by a blanket, Gladys had only days left. One of her three small children was crying as we entered her hut. Cradling Gladys's head in my arms, I bathed her face and helped her to take a few sips of water. Calling the children to her, the *vatete* hugged them, while I spoke gently to their mum: 'Jesus has sent us to tell you that he loves you. We're here to show you that you're special to him. He died for you, so that your sins can be forgiven. He came back to life, and his Spirit lives in people who believe in him. Jesus is God's very own Son. He wants to adopt you as his daughter and to give you a new life with him that will last for ever. This need not be the end, but the beginning.'

In some indefinable way, we were the 'fragrance of life' to that little girl and her family, even as they faced death.

Gladys's face became calm and peaceful, and the children stopped crying. We were on holy ground.

Afterwards, Bryan noticed that one of the little girls kept sniffing the hand that I had held, and he asked her why she was doing that. 'I can smell Jesus,' she replied. That seems a very strange thing to say, but 2 Corinthians 2:15 says, 'For we are to God the aroma of Christ among those who are being saved and those who are perishing. To the one we are the smell of death; to the other, the fragrance of life.' In some indefinable way, we were the 'fragrance of life' to that little girl and her family, even as they faced death.

On our way home, Bryan broke down in tears and continued to weep in the evening. In an article for his church magazine, he later wrote, 'Why this transformation? Why, in all the sadness and ugliness of this situation, did I feel a sense of privilege in being there, giving me tears of joy? It was nothing less than God's Holy Spirit filling the hut in such a tangible way. The Word becoming flesh by his Spirit – through his own people. What a wonderful, humbling experience.' His visit to Gladys was to make an impact on Bryan and his work at SGM for the next ten years, and it continues to motivate his passion to help children at risk in his retirement.

That night I cooked *sadza*, tomatoes and spinach in peanut butter, and, as we shared supper, Bryan revealed the main purpose of his visit. 'Scripture Gift Mission is starting a new range of Bible booklets for children in need, like street children and orphans. We need a consultant to help with the production of this new range. We'd like you to help us. It may entail overseas visits and helping to produce culturally appropriate literature that Christian workers can use as tools for the healing and restoration of the children.'

I looked at him in silence and amazement. Was this part of the picture that Bob had described, as he saw the veil to the future being lifted at one of its corners? As with Bob's letter, I simply promised Bryan that I would think and pray about what he had said, but I knew in my heart that our time in Zimbabwe would be coming to a close the following year. God was moving us on.

Next morning, I drove Bryan the one-and-a-half-hour journey to Masvingo, where we met with a coachload of SGM Directors from all over the world, who had come to pick Bryan up. 'Come and have a Coca Cola with us,' suggested Hugh Davies, the International Director. 'We've heard about you and your work.' Little did I know that I was being 'checked out', to see whether I would be suitable to help with the envisioned work with orphans and street children! I later learned that, as Hugh climbed into the coach on their departure, he turned to Bryan and said, 'She's the one.'

There was now no doubt in our minds. We would be leaving Zvishavane that summer. Since starting up The Bethany Project, I had groomed the team, and had worked in such a way that it could continue, with or without me. Local churches and communities had been mobilized to nurture and protect their own children; local governmental and non-governmental organizations had been brought together to respond more effectively to the needs of orphans and vulnerable children, and there was now greater advocacy on their behalf. Heather, Martha, Patience and the *vatetes* were confident in their roles, and enjoyed the oversight of a governing board committed to developing the work of the project. Now was the time to let go. From then on, I took a back seat, while encouraging Heather and the team to take the lead.

Finally in May 1998, the time came to leave. Every group of villages in each ward had to be visited so we could say 'farewell'. By then, The Bethany Project had mobilized around 200 villages, and was helping to support nearly 3,000 orphans and vulnerable children. Wherever I went, I met with intense sorrow and a total lack of comprehension as to why I was leaving. The depth of love expressed in speech after speech overwhelmed me. One old woman rose stiffly to her feet. Taking my hands, she looked into my eyes as she spoke in a cracked voice, 'When you first arrived in our villages, the children ran away from you. We all thought that you were a spirit, but the question we asked ourselves was, "Is she an evil or a good spirit?" Now we know that you are not a spirit, but that you are one of us. You are

You are white on the outside, but if we were to cut your skin, we would find that you are a black African on the inside.

white on the outside, but if we were to cut your skin, we would find that you are a black African on the inside. You have become a mother to our children, and a daughter to each one of us. As a member of our family, you can never be a stranger. Come back to us one day. Your home is here with us.'

Leaving Zvishavane was one of the hardest things I have ever done in my life. It's hard to describe just how much I had grown to love those people, and even the battered backwater town itself. It was as though God had taken a piece of his heart and grafted it into mine. Every 'goodbye' wrenched my being. I managed to hold myself together, until the final moment when we had to take Choux-Choux in a cardboard box to Heather and her family, who were going to look after him. Scrabbling away, he managed to burst out of the box as we were driving along, and started up a plaintive wail. His cry reflected my own pain. I sobbed uncontrollably. How could God be asking this of us?

Driving out of town for the last time, Jem and I felt numb and exhausted. It was a relief to be going to stay with Gary, Beryl and Bridget Strong who had become like family to us. Every few months, we had visited them in Harare for a break, and had always returned to Zvishavane restored by their love and kindness and 'Mum B's' fabulous home cooking! Now they gave us a place of sanctuary in their lovely home, where we were able to rest and recuperate before returning to the UK. Departing from Zimbabwe entailed wading through almost as much red tape as we had had to negotiate upon arrival. Our departure was therefore mercifully delayed by a couple of months, during which time we were able to start to make the mental and emotional transition from life in Zvishavane back to life in the UK. We luxuriated in having free time to visit our friends, Maurice and Wendy Adams and Tim and Sarah Dehn. Maurice had been my CEO at ACET after Patrick Dixon, and was now

Director for Zimbabwe for Voluntary Service Overseas (VSO). Tim was working for FEBA Christian radio. They and their families had frequently opened their hearts and homes to us in the preceding years, and, relaxing again with them now, we enjoyed being able to share English humour and precious time doing nothing in particular in the company of good friends.

Looking to the future, we had no idea of what lay ahead. We had no jobs to go to, no home and very little money. Most of our possessions had been sold in order to supplement Jem's small allowance during our time in Zvishavane. However, both of us knew beyond any shadow of a doubt that we could rely totally on our Heavenly Father, whose faithfulness, power and goodness we had experienced time and time again. The words of Isaiah 26:3 had become a living reality to us:

> You will keep in perfect peace
>> those whose minds are steadfast,
>> because they trust in you.
> Trust in the LORD for ever,
>> for the LORD, the LORD, is the Rock eternal.

We were returning to the UK in response to his calling. He would take care of us and reveal the next steps.

9. Holding up their arms

Large yellow ribbons were tied to every branch of the tree in the front garden, and 'Welcome Home' banners festooned windows and doorways, as Jane and my brother-in-law, David, pulled into their driveway, having picked us up from Heathrow Airport. Their home in Wokingham would be ours too for as long as we needed it.

Our first few days in the UK passed in a blur of hugs, laughter and joyful reunions with friends and family. Everything seemed slightly 'foreign'. The thick wool carpet in the living room felt alien to my feet, and, as I lay in bed on our first night back, the silence kept me awake. We had become used to the hypnotic rhythm of the piped marimba music and the drunken shouts and laughter emanating from the beer halls of Mandava Township in Zvishavane, until four some mornings. Now the silence felt vaguely threatening.

Adapting to being back in the UK was more of a shock than learning to live in Zimbabwe. The hours spent waiting in interminable post office queues in Zvishavane created golden opportunities to indulge in that most African of activities: chatting to one's neighbour. By comparison, the service in the post office in Wokingham was alarmingly speedy and efficient, and no-one in the queue would so much as look me in the eye, let alone engage in conversation. The supermarket left me feeling overwhelmed and inexplicably nauseated by the sheer choice of food and goods. It was like having to learn my own language and culture all over again, and, for the first few weeks, I felt like a wobbly beginner who needed stabilizers on her bike.

I had planned to spend two or three months just resting, and praying for God to show me the next step, but his timescale was obviously more European than African! After the first week back, I had a call from Bryan Stonehouse. 'Could you come up to London to meet with the team at Scripture Gift Mission? We'd like to continue the chat that we started in November.' By the end of the meeting with Bryan, Hugh Davies and David Atkinson, SGM's Publishing Director, I had been offered a brand new challenge: to set up from scratch a new project under SGM that would produce Bible-based resources to restore street children. 'We want to give you full freedom, and the time and support that you need, to continue to develop your work with The Bethany Project,' Bryan had generously said. 'The two roles need not be mutually exclusive.' Jeremy and I prayed about it, and, a couple of weeks later, I rang Bryan to accept the post of Director of the new project. My ex-youth leader would now become my 'boss'!

In exactly one month I was due to start at SGM and, during this time, I spent a lot of time thinking and praying about The Bethany Project. 'Was that it?' I asked God one day, as I prayed in Jane and David's spare room, 'or is there more?' I could almost hear laughter in God's voice as I felt him reply, 'Oh no! That was just the trial run! There's a lot more to come.' My heart sank somewhat! If that was just the trial run, then what on earth was to come? I felt that I had given blood at 'Bethany'. What more would be required of me? I was soon to find out.

As I prayed, a picture came to my mind of the priests Aaron and Hur holding up the arms of Moses during the battle between the Israelites and the Amalekites, described in Exodus 17:8–13. Moses was standing on a hilltop over-looking the battle. As long as he held his hands aloft to God, the Israelites were winning, but, as he became weary and lowered his hands, the Amalekites were on the front foot. Aaron and Hur sat Moses on a stone, and, standing on either side of him, they held up his arms, so that Israel was able to win the battle.

I did not make a habit of thinking about Moses, and I had rarely read this story. I knew that God was speaking through the picture, and I asked him what it meant. 'There is a battle going on in the lives of my children,' he replied. 'I want you to help mobilize my church to "hold up the arms" of those at the coalface of caring for children at risk, so that they have the support and strength they need to win the battle.' In the days that followed, I prayed more about this, and, as I did so, a strategy started to emerge, and with it a plan of action.

Working with The Bethany Project, I knew what it was like to labour at the cutting edge with children at risk. Every day, we had given out to those facing sickness, death and grief, in an environment of great deprivation. Of course, each day had also had its fair share of good things to celebrate. However, there had been times when the nature of the work had taken its toll, and we would have given anything for someone to come and 'hold up' *our* arms.

I would therefore start a charity in the UK that would mobilize and equip churches to respond to the needs of children at risk. On the one hand, the envisioned charity would 'hold up the arms' of Christian projects and workers caring for such children in different parts of the world, by serving them in any way that would make them more effective in fulfilling their vision. We would offer them bespoke training, information resources, and financial and prayer support. Through partnership with them, we would be able to achieve more together than apart. On the other hand, we would also mobilize churches in the UK and elsewhere to 'hold up the arms' of those in other parts of the world at the coalface of caring for vulnerable children. The more I thought and prayed about it, the more the vision blossomed and grew. Jesus once said, 'Apart from me you can do nothing' (John 15:5). I was more than aware of that. Experience had shown me that my part was simply to obey and remain rooted in him, and he would do the rest. God had no limitations. The word 'impossible' was not in his dictionary, so it wouldn't be in mine either.

I knew exactly whom I wanted with me in this new venture: Jan and Luke Wickings. By September 1998, Jan, Luke, Jane and I were sitting at Jane's dining table, having our first committee meeting, generously fuelled by prayer, coffee and chocolate biscuits. I had known Jan since she was a teenager, as she and Jane had attended the same church. She too had trained at St Thomas' Hospital and had become an HIV nurse specialist. She had married Luke, a church leader. They became loyal supporters of The Bethany Project, and Jem and I were thrilled when they came to visit us in Zvishavane with their lovely, young daughter, Hannah, and our beautiful god-daughter, Sarah, who had been born just a few days before we had left the UK for Zimbabwe. Jan and Luke's visit to Zvishavane had had a life-changing impact on them, and, when I asked them to help me set up the new charity, they didn't hesitate. Now here we were, excitedly discussing how to engage the hearts of Christians in the UK with what God was doing through his people in Zvishavane and beyond! Luke would be Chairman, Jane the Admin-istrator, and Jan and I trustees. By the time Jane had added the last full stop to the minutes, The Bethany Children's Trust (BCT) had been born!

For the next couple of years I worked flat out, devoting my time to developing the SGM street children's project during the day, and BCT-related work in the evenings, at weekends and during holidays. Jem and I needed to live nearer London so that I could save time travelling to SGM. For a few months we lived a nomadic existence, staying in the homes of whoever would have us, while we tried to find a home of our own. My BCT 'office' was wherever we happened to be living at the time. Ringing my old friend, Janni, in December 1998, I asked if we could stay with her and her young daughter, Sarah, for a couple of weeks. Six months later we were still camped in her spare room! Jem and I were grateful to her for being there for us at this rootless stage in our lives. Jesus said, 'Remain in me, and I will remain in you' (John 15:4), and, in a very real sense, he was our 'home' and our total security. We had absolute peace.

Around that time, I happened to come across a leaflet advertising The Cutting Edge Conference that was being run by an organization called Viva Network. My heart beat faster as I read the blurb. It transpired that Viva brought together Christian projects working with children at risk from around the globe in order to enhance their effectiveness and impact. Attending that conference was manna from heaven for me. Leading childcare practitioners working in some of the most challenging places on the planet shared their experiences with authority and humility, while I 'sat at their feet'. South and North Americans, Africans, Asians and Europeans came to debate, listen, learn, pray and eat together. As we did so, strong, lasting relationships and working partnerships emerged that would powerfully impact on the lives of vulnerable children around the world.

I was like a child let loose in a sweetshop! For the previous three years I had worked pretty much in isolation. Now, a whole new world of Christian childcare had opened before me, and I hungrily absorbed teaching and information that helped to stimulate my vision and understanding. My heart thrilled as I listened to the extraordinarily gifted and charismatic Patrick McDonald, Viva Network's Founding Director. 'Our task,' he challenged, 'is that the church, as a passionate advocate for children, might lead the world in their nurture and defence, so that every child has an opportunity to become all that God intended.' That was my kind of language! It was as though he was reading from a script that God had already written on my heart. The Bethany Children's Trust was a baby, but, as we linked hands with other organizations that shared a common vision, we were able to stand on the shoulders of giants and punch way above our weight.

One of those 'giants' at the conference was a diminutive, blonde-haired American called Heidi Baker. She was a spiritual tour de force, who stopped at nothing to preach the gospel fearlessly and rescue orphans and abandoned children from the streets and rubbish dumps of Maputo, the capital city of Mozambique. As Directors of Iris Ministries, Heidi and her husband, Rolland, had started to reach out to the poor and plant churches all over the nation. When terrible floods hit Mozambique, Iris Ministries put out an SOS. BCT mobilized teams of builders, electricians, plumbers and doctors from the UK to work alongside Iris Ministries, as they built dormitories and rescued children whose homes and families had been swept away by the deluge. BCT's partnership with Iris would continue over a number of years, as we helped to train Mozambican pastors in HIV care and prevention, and to fund and support a unit for abandoned babies and those living with HIV run by Iris Ministries at Zimpeto.

One of my abiding memories is of a morning spent with Heidi on a huge rubbish tip in Maputo, crawling with men, women and children, whose survival depended on what they could scavenge each day. Like some terrible scene from Dante's *Inferno*, tiny children picked their way through mounds of burning, rotting refuse, while flames licked around them. Human forms 'shimmered' like mirages in the heat, but these were flesh-and-blood people whom poverty had trodden underfoot. I staggered behind Heidi, dishevelled and choked by the smoke and fumes, while she daintily picked her way through the debris in sandals, her hair perfectly coiffured, a veritable vision in her red silk wrap, black leotard top and gold earrings. Now and again she stopped to chat and pray with a stooped, care-worn woman or a smoke-blackened child, and to share laughter and hugs with them.

'You still look amazing,' I commented afterwards, as we slaked our thirst with ice-cold drinks in a Maputo café. 'Do you always dress up for a visit to the tip?' Her reply has stayed with me ever since. 'These people are royal people, created in the image of God. I dress up for them, as I would for any member of a royal family.'

Tens of millions of children live in the world's sewers, streets and gutters: an indictment upon humanity if ever there was one.

'Princes and princesses' are not the names the world gives to children like those living off the rubbish tip and on the streets of Maputo. In Costa Rica, street children are called *chapulines* ('grasshoppers'), because they are perceived to be societal parasites that can be stepped on and crushed without thinking twice. In Colombia they are called *desechables*, meaning 'throwaways'. In the next few years, my work with BCT and SGM would find me sitting in the gutter with many a street child, and campaigning vigorously on their behalf. Tens of millions of children live in the world's sewers, streets and gutters: an indictment upon humanity if ever there was one. Poverty, AIDS, abusive home situations or rural-to-urban migration cause many children to end up on the streets, where they learn to survive by fair means or foul. Others run to the streets believing that they will find fortune and freedom, only to find themselves entrapped in an underbelly world where violence, hunger and abuse are daily realities.

In Zvishavane, Jeremy and I had opened our home to street children who lived by their wits in the local Mandava Bus Station. Wet footprints would pattern our floors as a gang of street boys revelled in the showers, hot food and change of clothing. It moved me intensely to watch these toughened boys playing with Super Ted, a large, stuffed bear with a knitted blue jacket, or the solemn way in which they would shut their eyes and fold their hands when we prayed with them. I loved these boys whom so many despised. They weren't little angels, but they were loyal, resourceful, and hungry to be loved and to belong. On one occasion, I was walking along the road in Zvishavane, when one of the street boys ran up and joyfully thrust his hand into mine. A passing pastor roughly pushed him aside. 'Go away!' he scolded. 'Don't bother Amai Howe!' 'Why did you do that?' I protested, angrily rounding on him. 'Because he is nobody,' was his appalling response. By the time I had finished with him, that pastor deeply regretted those words.

In part, it was this experience that had led me to accept my new role at SGM. I was determined to play a part in helping street children to see that they are 'somebody', and to raise awareness of their plight. Sitting on a train on my way to work one day, I was praying that God would give me a name for SGM's new project. My fellow commuters were reading their morning papers or dozing like nodding puppets, as the carriage swayed soporifically from side to side. As we passed the iconoclastic shell of the old Battersea Power Station, a picture came to my mind of a tiny red flower pushing its way through a crack in the pavement, a sign of life and beauty in a concrete jungle. That was it! We would call it 'Pavement Project', and the red flower would become the project logo.

Soon I had a fantastic team working with me. Gundelina Velazco was a professor of child psychology from the Philippines, whose advice and input were vital if we were to produce resources that would effectively help to bring psychological healing and restoration to traumatized street children. Isabelle Rosin had been a BBC producer who had worked with street children in Brazil. Andrea Thomas was a phenomenally creative ex-teacher who constantly had us thinking 'outside the box'.

According to Gundelina, one of the biggest effects of street life was upon the child's sense of self-worth. Abuse, abandonment and rejection destroy any feelings of esteem, causing a downward spiral in behaviour and the attrition of hope. Our starting place therefore would be to produce Bible-based resources that would help to restore self-worth.

SGM had bravely given us a blank sheet of paper to work from. Their original vision was to pilot the production of Bible booklets designed to bring hope to disaffected youth on the streets of inner cities in Scotland, but I had felt that we should greatly enlarge that vision. 'Let's go to the poorest of the poor and those at the bottom of the barrel,' I enthused to the leadership team as they eyed me cautiously across the table at one of our initial meetings. 'I suggest we do some pilot research in Asia, Africa and Latin America. Let's find out about the issues that street children have to deal with, and the effect that street life has upon them. Once we have a better understanding, we can start to produce relevant resources. On the whole, street children cannot read, so let's see what happens if we try to communicate with them through games, pictures and puppets.'

For over 100 years, SGM had only ever produced Scripture booklets. The recommendations of my team were a complete departure. It's a testament to their trust that the directors gave us the go-ahead. Ultimately, Pavement Project would radically impact on all other aspects of SGM's work and lead them to use an innovative and creative range of means, media and resources to communicate the Bible's message to ordinary men, women and children around the globe.[1]

Spring 1999 found me walking through a busy Manila marketplace in the middle of the day with a street worker called Bing. At the Cutting Edge Conference, I had met with leaders of the Philippines Child Ministry Network and, through them, was introduced to several Christian street ministries that would help with research. At the same time, BCT had started to partner with a wonderful ministry called 'Kanlungan Sa Erma', that was running a shelter for street children in a red-light district of Manila. Bing was one of Kanlungan's workers. As we walked together, his thick, black hair lay on his head like an oil slick, and sweat trickled in rivulets down his young face. The smog and humidity of Manila's polluted atmosphere smothered my airways like a thick blanket, making the smallest movement an effort.

'Let's go this way,' suggested Bing, as he led me past rickety, wooden trestle tables piled high with fragrant, exotic-looking fruits, set like jewels against dark green leaves. The market heaved with people frenetically buying and selling, all intent on getting the best possible deal. Garishly painted *tuk tuks* and rickshaws created havoc as they recklessly cut swathes through the crowds, blithely ignoring any rule of law.

'Here we are,' announced Bing, as we turned into a quiet, narrow alleyway, in which stood a couple of beige cardboard boxes the size of packing crates. 'Open it,' said Bing, pointing at one of the boxes. 'I can't do that,' I protested. 'It belongs to somebody.' 'Trust me,' Bing replied. Pulling up the lid of the box, I gasped in shock and amazement. Inside was a small boy, possibly nine years of age, curled up in a foetal position, his knees tucked under his chin, sleeping soundly. 'What on earth is he doing in there?' I asked naively, unable to believe my own eyes. 'That's his home,' said Bing, with that familiar shrug of the shoulders that I had seen again and again among people working with children at risk. A universal shrug that says, 'It's inexplicable.'

One of the hardest things was communicating what I had encountered during my increasingly frequent overseas visits to colleagues, family, friends and supporters of SGM and BCT. It was like living in two very different worlds. In Britain, our individualistic, consumerist society focuses on 'my rights', 'my needs', 'my comforts', and has a tendency to assume that 'everyone is like us', or at least to wish it were so. Even some parts of the church have held on to an inward-looking mentality, leading to a massive ignorance of what life is like for the majority of people in the world, for whom survival is a hand-to-mouth, slippery affair, like walking on thin ice.

Increasingly, I began to speak in churches, schools and groups in the UK, trying to paint a picture of a world where young children have to scavenge barefoot on burning rubbish tips in order to survive, or sleep like dogs in back alleyways, with nothing more than a flimsy piece of cardboard to protect them. It wasn't money that I wanted from those I spoke to, but their hearts and practical action. The words of Lamentations 2:19 acted as a rallying cry:

> Arise, cry out in the night,
> as the watches of the night begin;
> pour out your heart like water
> in the presence of the Lord.
> Lift up your hands to him
> for the lives of your children,
> who faint from hunger
> at the head of every street.

By December 1999, Jem and I had learned to stop greeting people in Shona, and no longer expected strangers to say 'hello' to us when they passed us in the street. We had happily settled into our little one-bedroom flat in Putney with its small patch of garden, and we loved our octogenarian neighbours, 'old John' downstairs, and 'old Charlie' next door. They quarrelled terribly at times, but were firm friends who shared a mutual passion for growing roses and tomatoes, and drinking cups of tea.

Jem was working two days a week as a pharmacy inspector for the health authority, and assisted Bob at the Community Church in Putney one day a week. The rest of Jem's time was spent studying for a masters degree in Health Systems Management at the School for Tropical Diseases, and renovating our flat with the help of 'Papa', my great stepdad, who was converting what had originally been a slum into our ideal home.

The Bethany Children's Trust was now a registered charity, and going from strength to strength, as we provided information, resources, funding, prayer and training support to our three project partners: Kanlungan, Iris Ministries and The Bethany Project. Our support base was growing too, and I had a full speaking schedule. In fact, I was starting to wonder how long I could continue to balance my increasing responsibilities with SGM and BCT.

My greatest passion was to see the church authentically demonstrating the character of Christ and his kingdom, and fulfilling its mandate to 'Seek justice, encourage the oppressed. Defend the cause of the fatherless, plead the case of the widow' (Isaiah 1:17). I didn't hesitate, therefore, to accept an invitation at this time to attend and speak at a conference in Namugongo, Uganda, that was being organized by the Judah Trust. The purpose of the event was to mobilize church leaders in Uganda to become actively involved in HIV care and prevention, and I was to speak on the community-based care of orphans and vulnerable children. The conference was to prove pivotal for many reasons, not least because it was there that I would meet exceptional men and women of calling, calibre and commitment, who were sacrificially caring for people living with HIV in different parts of the world, alongside whom I would work in time to come.

The day came for me to deliver my talk. The air was still, the morning bright and expectant. It was that lovely, fresh time in an African day, before the heat of the sun saps air and energy, making it necessary to move in slow motion. Open windows looked out over the quadrangle of the training centre that had been loaned to us for the duration of the conference. Having been introduced by Reverend Ray Thomas, who leads Judah Trust with his wife Joy, I walked to the front, sensing the familiar frisson of nerves in my stomach that I always experience immediately before giving an address. Just as I was about to open my mouth, God broke powerfully into my line of thought: 'I have given you a trumpet to blow, to call my church to rise up and care for orphans, the vulnerable and the outcasts,' he said. 'In exactly a year from now, I want you to leave SGM and start working full-time for The Bethany Children's Trust. You are to blow the trumpet that I have given you.'

Anyone reading this who has not yet heard the voice of God may understandably write me off as being of unsound mind. Others will fully understand, because they too have come to recognize the voice of the one who may speak in a whisper, deep in the inner recesses of our hearts, or communicate through dreams and visions. As Peter quotes in Acts 2:17–18:

In the last days, God says,
    I will pour out my Spirit on all people.

Your sons and daughters will prophesy,
    your young men will see visions,
    and your old men will dream dreams.
Even on my servants, both men and women,
    I will pour out my Spirit in those days,
    and they will prophesy.

Standing there in the conference centre, I knew without a shadow of a doubt that God had spoken, and, when God speaks, I've learned that it's a good idea to listen – carefully. Psalm 95:7–8 says, 'Today, if you hear his voice, do not harden your hearts . . .' However, this was not exactly great timing on God's part. 'With respect, can we talk about this later?' I prayed under my breath. 'All these people are waiting for me to start.'

I managed to get into my stride and give the talk that I had prepared. Many came up afterwards to say how affected they were by what they had heard. I was later to learn that, as a result of the talk, a couple of people were challenged to start working with street children, and another couple stepped out to start training churches in HIV care and prevention. As the participants trailed out for the tea break, Ray Thomas quietly walked up and drew me aside. 'As you spoke, Susie, I believe that God gave me a word for you,' he gently confided. 'He has given you a trumpet, and you are to blow it. I believe that you are to be a voice to the church, calling it out of complacency, and to be the church that reflects the character of Christ.' Once again, I was rendered speechless. 'I know,' I acknowledged. 'He's just told me.' I went to my room to think and pray.

Leaving SGM to work for BCT would mean going unsalaried. Jem had only two days' paid work a week, and we had a mortgage and other outgoings. And what about the work at SGM? We were at the stage of starting to develop and try out prototype resources, and beginning to set up

Pavement Project bases in Asia, Africa and Latin America. How could I just walk out? On my return home, Jem's response when I shared with him what had happened was typically wise and supportive: 'Let's pray about this together and ask God to give clear confirmation that it is right. If we get confirmation, we will know that God will take care of us and of SGM, no matter what.'

We told absolutely no-one about what had happened, and quietly prayed about it together. Three months later, our phone rang. It was our Pastor, Bob. 'Graham and I would like to pop round to see you,' he said. 'Would tomorrow night be OK?' The next evening found Bob, and Graham, one of our church leaders, sitting on our couch, with Jem and me sitting opposite them, wondering what on earth they had come to talk to us about. Looking directly at me, Bob came straight to the point. 'You are called to lead The Bethany Children's Trust forward. This isn't a little part-time job that you can do on the side. It's a mantle that God has given you which requires your full energy and commitment. Graham and I have talked and prayed about this together, and we both feel that you should work full-time for The Bethany Children's Trust. We'll set up a fully-equipped office at the church for you to work from, with no rent or costs, and, as a church, we'll do all we can to support the work that God has called you to.'

We didn't need any further confirmation! Nine months later, in December 2000, exactly a year after God had spoken to me in Namugongo, I opened the door to my new BCT office with its newly-painted yellow walls, and sat at my computer as full-time Director of The Bethany Children's Trust. As I did so, part of the ceiling fell in, covering the computer and me with plaster and water from a hidden leak.

Sitting there alone, on that cold December morning, I had no idea of just how far God was going to take me with BCT, or of the extraordinary impact it was to have on the lives of thousands of children in many, many countries. All I knew was that my clothes were soaked and my hair was full of debris. I had started this new phase of my life with a bang, or perhaps a damp squib would be more accurate! Laughing, I tried to clean up the mess. Working for BCT was obviously not going to be without its challenges, but I was up for whatever lay ahead!

10. Breaking the silence

Stepping into Ntarama Church in Rwanda was like stepping into some tortured scene from Hieronymus Bosch's imagery of hell. Bones were piled high in one corner: a mismatched jumble of tibias and femurs, crushed skulls and pelvises, like pieces from an enormous anatomy puzzle that needed putting together. Around the bare room lay innumerable skeletons of all sizes, collapsed over one another. Tattered rags of faded blouses and shorts, muddied wraps and flip-flops lay scattered and mouldering among the remains. Here was a red, plastic beaker, and there a pale blue tin plate rusting next to a gaping skull. Most poignant of all was a lined schoolbook thrown to the ground, with a child's writing looping across the open page in grey pencil. In the far, red-brick wall, a hole had been blasted, through which I could see graceful banana trees growing in the church grounds, their broad, flat leaves lit up by the dazzling sunshine, like a tantalizing glimpse of paradise as seen from Sheol.

I stood in deep silence with Francis Mutabazi, the leader of AIDS Prevention Care Outreach Ministry (APRECOM), BCT's latest partner project in Rwanda. It was October 2001. Standing in that terrible place, the full horror of the 1994 Rwandan genocide hit me with sickening force. Hundreds of people seeking shelter inside the church had been slaughtered seven years previously, when members of the Interahamwe militia had locked the doors and fired in shells of ammunition. Those who didn't die from the explosions were hacked to death with machetes, every last man, woman and child. Altogether, around 5,000 people were killed in the villages of Ntarama. The church building had been left untouched, bearing silent testimony to the unthinkable.

This was my first visit to Rwanda. I had met Francis at the Namugongo conference nearly two years previously. A man of exceptional ability and great compassion, he and his wife, Dorothy, had been raised in Uganda as part of the Rwandan Diaspora, and had chosen to return to Rwanda immediately after the genocide, like many Rwandans, to help rebuild their shattered country. Subsequently, they had helped to set up APRECOM in the capital city of Kigali, to care for families affected by HIV, as part of Youth With A Mission (YWAM) ministries. Around 11% of the population were HIV-positive, some as a consequence of having been raped in the genocide. The entire nation was still in trauma, while determinedly trying to recreate itself. 'Please come and help us,' Francis had said. 'We have an overwhelming task on our hands.' So I had come to listen, learn, and help run a training workshop for church leaders in HIV awareness and care. I had read as much as I could about Rwanda, and about the genocide and its impact, in order to be more fully prepared for issues that might be raised. Now, here I was with Francis, numbly trying to comprehend what I was seeing with my own eyes.

Running the four-day workshop was sheer joy, partly because of the sterling team I was part of. Francis, Dorothy and I taught with Richard and Prilla Rowlands from the UK. Richard was a doctor, and Prilla an HIV educator, whom we had also met at Namugongo. This gentle couple had previously lived and worked in Rwanda for twelve years and spoke fluent Kinyarwandan. Prisca Mukinisha, Francis and Dorothy's colleague, was a powerful and gifted communicator.

Stigma and discrimination against those living with HIV was rife in Rwanda in general, and also in the church, and decades of internecine hatred and unforgiveness had affected everyone. The workshop brought together church pastors and leaders of women's and youth groups from Hutu and Tutsi backgrounds, the two main ethnic groups of Rwanda. All of them had lost family, colleagues, neighbours and friends seven years previously, when extremist Hutus had massacred an estimated 800,000 Tutsis and moderate Hutus in the 100 days of terror. Now, here we were, asking those participating in the workshop to love and care for their HIV-infected neighbour – whether Hutu or Tutsi. We were totally reliant on the work of the Holy Spirit to transform hearts and minds.

Our starting place was to teach about our shared identity as God's people, and the culture of God's kingdom. As we taught, beliefs and attitudes were realigned with the Word of God. Using role-play and group discussions, we shared about HIV awareness and care. The story of the Good Samaritan came alive as never before, as we examined it in the context of Rwanda. 'Who is my neighbour?' enquired the expert in the law as he tried to test Jesus, as described in Luke 10. This was the question that every Rwandan was asking. Since the 100 days of national insanity, no-one really knew any more. Those present at the workshop needed to learn, as did the expert in the law, that Christ's law requires us to show mercy, even to those considered our enemies, regardless of ethnicity and past hurts and offences.

The impact of this initial workshop was extraordinary. At one stage, people wept openly together. 'I hated you when I first arrived,' said a tall, handsome-looking woman, pointing at me. 'The United Nations turned its back on us during the genocide, and ran away. In my mind, you represented the whites who abandoned us to our fate and ignored our pleas for help. But I have watched and listened to you over these past few days, and God has changed my heart. Now I feel free, and I can honestly say that I love you.'

Hutus and Tutsis asked one another for forgiveness, and received it. New friendships were forged, and those present went back to their churches to pass on to others what they had learned. Again and again, in our future training workshops, we were to encounter the Holy Spirit at work, healing hearts, minds, attitudes and relationships, and enabling us to go way beyond a simple teaching and training programme.

Six months later, at the invitation of Bishop Augustin Mvunabandi, I returned with Prilla and Richard to Rwanda to help the APRECOM team with further training workshops in Kigeme, a place of breathtaking beauty and sweeping, panoramic mountain scenery, in the south-west. 'AIDS is the new genocide,' the bishop had said. 'It is killing so many in our parishes. Please come and train my pastors and church leaders so that we can combat this disease.' As a result of that training, the diocese started a project called *Abisunzimana* ('He whose hope is in the Lord'). Tirelessly led by the bishop's wife, Madame Virginie Mukanziga, Abisunzimana mobilized teams of Christian volunteers to support those living with HIV in the undulating mountains and terraced villages of Kigeme.

Afterwards, with BCT's partnership, training and funding support, both APRECOM and Abisunzimana went on to develop home-based care programmes for those living with HIV, and dozens of adult and children's support groups, income-generating projects and anti-AIDS clubs were set up, impacting the lives of countless men, women and children. During frequent successive visits to Rwanda, I saw entire families and communities come alive. Despair was routed by faith and a living hope. In one APRECOM support group, a bright-eyed man stood up and said, 'I thank God that I became HIV-positive. Through it, I came to be cared for by APRECOM, and they led me to know and love the Lord Jesus Christ. Now I am alive as never before, and I am no longer afraid to die.'

My work with BCT took me increasingly to different African nations, as our network of partnerships grew and developed. By 2003, in addition to APRECOM, Abisunzimana, Iris Ministries and Kanlungan Sa Erma, BCT was also supporting Botshabelo, which cared for impoverished children and families with HIV in a township outside Johannesburg, Project Purpose, helping to bring young girls out of prostitution in Maputo, Mozambique, and White Eagle Boys, a church-led project rescuing boys from the streets in Masaka, Uganda.

Everything we did was underpinned by prayer. Heather Sandiford had become BCT's invaluable, volunteer Prayer Coordinator, helping me to produce our prayer diary, and leading a team of wonderful prayer partners, who were committed to praying for emergency situations that arose from time to time in the lives of the children and projects. Heather's husband, Geoff, gave his time and skills to designing and producing BCT's quarterly magazine. The Board of Trustees had grown in number, and I also had three fantastic colleagues working with me full time.[1]

In 2003, BCT discontinued active support of The Bethany Project, when we learned that it had been taken over by those whose motives were political and corrupt. It was incredibly hard to hear at the time, but we continued to pray that God would somehow restore what had been 'hijacked'. It was with joy that I received an email in 2007 from a wonderful woman called Jean Webster, to say that she and her team were going to start working with churches in Zvishavane, mobilizing them to care for and protect orphans and vulnerable children. Jeannie is a living legend who moved to Zimbabwe in the seventies and never left. She founded Zimbabwe Orphans through Extended Hands (ZOE), which has mobilized churches all over Zimbabwe to care for and support orphans and vulnerable children. I was thrilled to think that she and her team were picking up the baton that had been dropped.

In August 2003, Jeremy and I decided to attend Greenbelt, a Christian festival held in Cheltenham that was, and still is, the 'Glastonbury' of the Christian world! Armed with a tent, wellies and lots of body wipes, we made our way to the vast racecourse that was to be our temporary home for three days. I revelled in the music events and talks on justice by leading luminaries and well-known activists. 'You should come with me to the talk by Bishop Benjamin Ojwang,' recommended Jane Beckford, when I bumped into her in the milling crowds. 'He's going to speak on children who are being abducted in Northern Uganda by some rebel group.'

Jane was a senior infection-control nurse, a passionate BCT supporter and a member of our church. She had done a brilliant job of running an infection-control training workshop for the Iris Ministries' baby unit that BCT helped to support in Mozambique. On one hand, I fancied a weekend free of issues related to children at risk, but, on the other hand, Jane's comments intrigued me. I went along with her. The room was already packed when we arrived. As we sat on the floor at the back, a small, elderly man dressed in a dark, baggy suit was ushered to the front. This was 'Bishop Ben', as he was known, Bishop of the Diocese of Kitgum, Northern Uganda, a man of enormous courage and humility. What he had to share in his deceptively soft voice was powerful and shocking.

'In the past twenty years, the Lord's Resistance Army has abducted over 20,000 of our children in northern Uganda, forcing them to become child soldiers and sex slaves. Whole villages have been wiped out. There has been mass murder and torture, and over one million of my people are now living in sub-human conditions in refugee camps. Our government is doing little about it. If just one British child is abducted, there is public outrage, and the news hits the newspaper headlines. Over 20,000 of our children have been abducted, but there is universal silence from the international community. Are the children of my nation any less valuable than your children? For their sakes, I ask you to break the silence with me.'

The Church Mission Society had brought Bishop Ben to the UK, as part of their 'Break the Silence' campaign. Martin Luther King Junior once said, 'Our lives begin to end the day we become silent about things that matter.' I knew there and then that God was calling BCT to stand with the people of Northern Uganda, and to do what we could to help 'break the silence' too. In the year that followed, BCT conducted a prayer and advocacy campaign among our supporters and churches in the UK. We cried to God to bring justice to the people of northern Uganda and, through a petition campaign, urged the British government to put diplomatic pressure on the Ugandan government to protect its civilians and to act justly.

Are the children of my nation any less valuable than your children?

The response was encouraging, as many 'woke up' to what was happening and supported the campaign. But I wasn't satisfied. More had to be done. I wanted to go to northern Uganda as a representative of BCT to demonstrate our love and solidarity, and to show the people they were not forgotten. But how and where? A telephone call with Kate Muammar, whom I had met at that significant Namugongo conference, was the turning point. A lovely English woman with an intrepid spirit, she was bravely calling and equipping the church to respond to HIV disease in many parts of Africa where others feared to tread. 'Speak with Ann Emuron, who works for Global Care in Soroti,' Kate had recommended, when I shared my heart for northern Uganda with her. 'Ann is a good friend. She and her team are helping to run a camp for a hundred children who are separated from their families because of the Lord's Resistance Army. They really need help and support.' That was it! With the permission of BCT's trustees, I set off for north-east Uganda in May 2004, and found myself sitting on a bus in a crowded bus park in the capital city of Kampala, waiting to travel to Soroti.

The journey took us through dusty towns whose façades had long since seen better days, and beautiful countryside thick with fields of emerald sugar cane and banana plant-ations. Ann Emuron turned out to be a slim, middle-aged woman with a deep love for God and the children she was helping to care for. As we shared a cup of tea together, she reinforced all that Bishop Ben had described. 'It's as though Uganda is a country split into two nations,' she explained. 'The south is flourishing and peaceful, and the darling of donor agencies, while here in the north, we have known nothing but suffering for the past couple of decades. It wasn't until last year when the LRA advanced as far as Soroti that our government woke up. They realized that, unless the rebels were halted, they would reach Kampala. Government troops were mobilized and the rebels were pushed back. In all the chaos, several thousand people have been displaced here in Soroti and are now living in Internally Displaced People's camps.'

Global Care Uganda, the agency that Ann worked for, was running a child-sponsorship programme in Soroti. After the LRA had invaded the town, they had started to feed thousands of displaced children. 'We saw that some children were more vulnerable than others,' continued Ann, 'particu-larly the unaccompanied ones who were trying to fend for themselves. We set up a camp to shelter and care for one hundred of them.'

I visited the Global Care centre where the children were being looked after in brightly coloured tents. Thirteen-year-old Dickson was engrossed in a board game when I met him and other children from the centre. His clear eyes and smiling face belied what he had suffered. He and his father had been abducted by the LRA. On the first day, his father had been shot and killed. Dickson managed to escape, and made his way back home again. As he entered his thatched dwelling, he found the LRA had tied together his brother and sister on the ground, and then tried to set light to the hut. Although the thatched roof and walls were blackened, the fire had mysteriously burnt itself out. Dickson untied his brother and sister, and ran with them to safety. Now all the children were being cared for at Global Care's centre. Listening to Dickson quietly tell his story, my heart was anguished and outraged.

Visiting the Internally Displaced People's (IDP) camps with Ann was a real eye-opener, to put it mildly. Measuring around two miles in length, the first one that I visited housed thousands of adults and children. Row upon serried row of closely packed, thatched shelters stretched to the horizon. Only ten overflowing portable toilets and three water taps served the entire camp. 'I long to go home, but when I think of the terrible killings, I dread the thought,' shuddered one old woman. 'Thank you for coming to visit us,' said an old man, as I sat on the floor next to him. 'You're the first white person to actually stop and sit with us. Most of the aid agencies arrive in their four-wheel drive cars, take photos of us and then leave.' We moved from row to row, stopping here to chat with a gang of giggling children, and there to sit and talk with the elderly. It was a real joy to pray for several families and to share the hope of God's Word. 'You have brought us something memorable today,' said one old lady. 'We will not forget it. When we return to our villages, we will remember this day.'

The government was insisting that those in the camps should go back to their villages to resettle, and that included the hundred children in Global Care's centre. 'Once we have traced the children's relatives, we will help to build a hut for each family back in their villages, and give them "starter packs" of pots, pans, bedding, clothing and seeds,' said Ann. 'We will also continue to follow up the children and their guardians, giving them counselling and spiritual support.'

I wanted to see for myself what the children would be going back to and, with Ann's help, arranged a visit out to Olwa, one of the more remote areas that had been devastated by the LRA. Getting there was not easy. As the tracks became narrower, and then non-existent, we abandoned the van we were travelling in. Walking through the hot, dry bush, we were hit by the silence. Where once the air rang with village sounds – children laughing, neighbours calling to one another, and goats bleating – now there was simply the incessant buzzing of insects. Sometimes we would come across the derelict remains of a hut, wantonly burnt and destroyed by the rebels. As we ducked into the doorway of one abandoned hut, we could see the poignant remains of a rotting mattress and a couple of pieces of children's clothing, scattered on the floor, presumably dropped by the owners as they ran in fear. Where once there were cultivated fields and gardens, now there was just a dense tangle of tall grasses and undergrowth. One of the first tasks of returning villagers would be to clear the wilderness before attempting literally to rebuild their lives again, brick by brick, one hut at a time. They would need help.

That was it! Standing in that place of dereliction, a green shoot of a vision came to me of how we could play a part in bringing restoration. 'You could help to resettle just a hundred children and leave it at that,' I said to Ann excitedly,

Susie with EPED and Pukusu Children's Ministries workers, DR Congo, 2009

Top: Susie with a couple of children supported by
Botshabelo team, RSA, 2006
Bottom: Susie in the back of a truck after a motor breakdown
on the way to Abeko, northern Uganda, 2006

Susie, Henry and Collins, the Wukwashi Project, 2006

Top: Susie with a child in Kanlungan sa Erma, the Philippines
Bottom: Grace giving a ball to Derek, Wukwashi Project, 2007

Top: Forest homestead, Pukusu
Bottom: Susie and Josina, Rwanda, 2007

Top: Helping to train crèche teachers in a township in Midrand, RSA, with Botshabelo Team.
Bottom: In the Democratic Republic of Congo, 2009

Top: Radio interview, 2009
Bottom: Susie in the office of The Bethany Children's Trust, 2009

Susie and one of the girls from EPED's refuge, 2010

'*or* you could help to resettle them *and* restore entire communities. Identify an area that has no support from other agencies, where the people are willing to help themselves. Get the local people to assess what they and their children most need help with, in order to be able to start their lives over again. Then let's work with them to help make that happen.'

Thus began our partnership with Global Care and the people of Abeko Parish in the Amuria District. Together, we helped the population of 2,462 to re-establish their lives. Just fifty kilometres from Soroti, it nevertheless took two hours to get to Abeko, because the roads were almost impassable. In 2003, Abeko had been taken over by the LRA and used as a base for their operations, forcing local people to flee. The parish's wells had been vandalized by the rebels. Following a needs assessment with the returning local population, the greatest necessity was overwhelmingly perceived to be access to clean water and sanitation, to mitigate the high prevalence of water-borne diarrhoeal disease among local children.

Over the next few years, with BCT's support, Global Care helped the local villagers to build or repair six wells, a borehole and around 250 pit latrines, to help improve sanitation. Health-promotion groups were formed to help teach good hygiene, and ten child-support groups were established, providing several hundred children with play, friendship, counselling, income-generation projects, Bible teaching and spiritual support. Child-protection groups were established to act and advocate on behalf of children who were being abused, and to teach childcare and protection. Agricultural projects were initiated at the local primary school, and local churches were mobilized in childcare and protection.

Some of my favourite memories are of staying in Abeko Parish with members of the Global Care team. On my first visit in July 2006, the villagers were agog to see the *mzungu* (white person) who had arrived, along with Ann, and Alice, a Global Care volunteer. We had loaded up the hired car with water, bananas, sleeping mats, cooking pots and all the essentials for our stay. Upon reaching Abeko at dusk, a local church leader, Pastor Martin, proudly led us to a new mud hut that was to become our home for the next few days. We duly admired the fine grass thatching, held up by wooden poles and a central tree trunk. Darkness fell rapidly like a cloak around us, and we sat outside under the dense canopy of stars, enjoying the peace and watching the glowing fireflies as they danced sprite-like around us. Pastor Martin had been born in Abeko, and in his low voice he shared stories from his boyhood, as we cooked over a fire. Supper finished, and we took it in turns to have cold-water bucket washes under the stars, gratefully cleansing away the grime of the day. Everywhere was silent, and the sky had never looked so vast. Eventually we crawled gratefully under our mosquito nets and fell instantly fast asleep.

Over the following days, I walked from village to village, encouraging the local people, playing with the children, hearing their stories and learning about their lives. In the evenings, many would turn up at the door of our hut, curious to see what the *mzungu* looked like. They were amazed to discover that she not only appeared to be at home in the bush, but could even cook like an African woman over a fire, sweep a hut in the right way with a bundle of dried grass, and sleep on the floor as they did. I was amused to discover that news of what I was doing was relayed out across the villages by the very effective bush telegraph!

On our final morning, village elders gathered solemnly at our *manyatta* to say goodbye. 'Even our own people have not come as you have,' said one elder with broken teeth. 'You have come deep into the bush and lived with us. We have never known such a thing. Truly you have shown us God's love. Now you have a home here, and the door is open whenever you want to visit us.'

Since then, Abeko has started to flourish. Roads have been built into the area, and other agencies are joining hands with the local people. The villages have come alive again, and the children live in greater hope. The LRA have now moved their base from northern Uganda to the north of the Democratic Republic of Congo, where they are actively committing acts of violence and atrocities against civilians.

Sitting in the departures lounge of Entebbe Airport after that visit, I tried to prepare myself mentally for the next leg of my journey: a visit to Jos in Nigeria where I would meet up with Gill. Together we were going to help Scripture Union Western Africa to train church leaders from Sierra Leone, Liberia and Nigeria in HIV care and prevention and how to look after vulnerable children. From there, we were going on to Hear the Cry, a Viva Network Conference in Kenya, where we would meet with childcare workers from all over Africa to see how we could work together more effectively.

One opportunity after another was being opened up to BCT to call and equip the church to act and advocate on behalf of children at risk. Little did I know then that God would lead BCT into new areas, to confront issues that would be more challenging than anything we had yet encountered. The adventure had barely begun!

11. 'Is something special happening here today?'

It's February 2008. I'm sitting suspended high above the River Congo, squashed in the back of a tiny, four-seater plane and surrounded by cabbages and eggs. Far below, the khaki-coloured waters of the fabled river flow fat and sleek as far as my eye can see. The roar and whine of the engines is deafening, and, now and again, the plane drops suddenly, along with my stomach, as we hit a thermal.

Along with the groceries, I'm being flown by a Mission Aviation Fellowship pilot to a village in the interior of the Democratic Republic of Congo (DRC) called Bonga Yasa, along with Paul Kabanga, a jovial, easy-going man who works for Pukusu Children's Ministries. As we pass over mile upon mile of forest, bush and undulating hills, I reflect on the events that have brought me here.

It had all started during the Viva Network Hear the Cry Conference in 2004. We had recognized that, although development organizations were falling over themselves in eastern and southern Africa, there was a dearth of agencies willing to work alongside communities in western Africa, where instability and poor infrastructure and communications presented greater challenges, as did the fact that western Africa is francophone as opposed to anglophone.

Gill and I came away convinced that BCT should prayerfully look into working in western Africa. We even started French classes in preparation, making each other laugh as we tried to resuscitate our rusty schoolgirl French.

In 2005, BCT began to partner with Vie Nouvelle et Développement Intégral (VINODI), a wonderful, church-led programme for street children and those living with HIV, in a town called Tsevie, in Togo, western Africa. When we heard that Pastor Thomas, the visionary leader of VINODI, and other members of his church had sold their houses and land to start caring for those who were being treated as social outcasts, we knew that we wanted to join hands with them. Since then the work had really taken off. As we had seen before in other nations, the good news of the gospel was having a powerful effect on people in Tsevie and its surrounding villages, as it was being put into radical action.

In 2007 the Democratic Republic of Congo (DRC) came on to our radar. A pastor had written to me in the spring of that year asking BCT to consider partnering with a project that he and several other pastors were involved in, caring for street children and those with HIV around Kinshasa, the capital. His name was Pastor Ngolo, and the project was Equipe Pastorale auprès des Enfants en Détresse (EPED). BCT receives countless requests for help and support, but there was an indefinable something about this particular email that made it jump off the screen. By then, BCT had moved to offices in Teddington, Middlesex, Tom Green had moved on, as Dave Anns and Gill Grant would soon do also, and Claire Lanham had joined as our new Communications Coordinator. I showed her Pastor Ngolo's email and the accompanying proposal document written in elegant French. Something of the excellence, passion and integrity of the man and the project shone through.

For many, the DRC epitomizes all that is most tragic about the turbulent history of the African continent. Formerly known as the Congo Free State prior to Independence in 1960, and then Zaire, this vast nation and its people have suffered for centuries at the hands of brutal colonialists, avaricious and corrupt dictators, and the unscrupulous and at times murderous manipulations of foreign powers, whose leaders have been intent on protecting their own political and economic interests. Decades of civil war have left the nation on its knees.

And yet, there it was, that familiar leap in my spirit. There was nothing for it. We began to pray, and asked very specific-ally that God would confirm whether or not we were to work in the DRC. Before Pastor Ngolo's email, BCT had never been approached by agencies or individuals there. However, a couple of days later, I received a telephone call from Pastor Robert Grayson of Southfields Baptist Church in London. 'I don't know if you can help,' he started tentatively, 'but there's a Congolese man in my church whose father is a pastor in a place called Pukusu in the DRC. He and his church are trying to support 300 children who have been orphaned by war and disease. We have raised some funds to help them, but they need assistance in developing their work. Would BCT be prepared to get involved?'

So that was how I came to be circling in the plane above Bonga Yasa, before we finally touched down on a small, sandy landing strip in the middle of a large field. In response to Pastor Grayson's request, I was going to visit Pukusu Children's Ministries (PCM), before returning to Kinshasa to visit Pastor Ngolo and EPED.

Having spent the night at Bonga Yasa in the home of one of the villagers, we were ready to travel the seventy kilo-metres to Pukusu in a Land Rover lent to us by the local Catholic priest. The old warhorse of a vehicle proved its worth, as our driver negotiated deeply rutted tracks, narrow streams and steep inclines. Finally, we entered the outskirts of Pukusu, deep in the bush. As we slowed to a crawl, I was bemused to see that the narrow track was lined with hundreds of people blowing whistles, beating drums and singing at the tops of their voices. Men, women and children waved palm branches and danced with extraordinary energy and verve. Turning to Paul, I asked, 'Is something special happening here today?' 'Why, yes,' he replied. 'You have arrived.'

As we climbed down from the Landie, hot, dusty and dishevelled, a small, elderly man with quiet dignity stepped up to welcome us. It was Pastor Aaron Mizwa, the leader of PCM. Together we walked towards the village. Four men held a canopy over us, and, as we progressed, more and more villagers lined the route. Borne along on a sea of humanity, I wondered whether I had been mistaken for someone else. It was hard to comprehend the impact my visit seemed to be making.

Later that evening it became clear. I received a visit from two village chiefs, and asked them to describe the changes they had experienced in Pukusu during their reign of office. They answered rapidly, while Paul translated for me. 'There have been no real changes in our villages and no big events for over fifty years,' one said. 'The greatest event that has happened in our time has been your visit to us. For over fifty years even our own politicians have forgotten our community, but now someone has remembered us. You have come.' I couldn't help thinking what a disappointing figure I must have cut in the eyes of the villagers. They'd been waiting for half a century for someone to visit them, and who should turn up? A stick-thin woman with a bedraggled appearance and a complete lack of status! It was almost funny. 'I have come to learn from you,' I said. 'You have a lot to teach me.'

The following day, over a breakfast of delicious, fresh pineapple and sweetened tea, Pastor Mizwa explained how PCM had started. 'I saw the way that children were suffering and couldn't bear it. Every time I prayed for them, I would weep. It's as though God gave me a piece of his heart. The fathers of many of the children around here went to fight as soldiers in the east of the country and never returned. I started visiting the orphan children and their families, and praying for them. Then I decided that, as a church, we had to do something more, so two years ago we started PCM. Volunteers from the church visit orphan households to give friendship and support, and, with the help that comes from my son's church in the UK, we've been able to start paying for food for the most needy children and also their school fees. Now we need your help to take our work further.' I looked in admiration at this elderly man with his lined, leathery face and twisted, arthritic fingers. 'There's a real problem here,' he continued. 'People have endured so much hardship. It's as though they have lost the ability to feel compassion or any sense of motivation. We need to help them to rediscover it.'

After breakfast we set out to explore the village. Leading me to a large tract of impenetrable wilderness, Pastor Mizwa pointed out where he wanted to develop an agricultural project and fish farm with BCT's help, as a means of generating income for medical and school fees, and supplementing the nutrition of Pukusu's orphans and vulnerable children. I gazed at the dense wall of riotous jungle dubiously. Pastor Mizwa was definitely a man of vision. 'This land is very close to the river, so it's perfect for the projects I have in mind,' he said excitedly. 'With easily available water, anything is possible. Come, let me show you the river.'

The heat of the sun was grim, so it was a relief to enter the cool environment of the shaded forest, where lush, broad-leaved palms formed a welcome canopy, and a glorious riot of unrestrained vegetation and vines curled and entwined around everything in their path. Ebony trees towered above us, and here and there we discovered coffee plants with luminous, white flowers and a glorious, heavy scent that sensually pervaded the air. Occasionally we came across a clearing where one or two families had built homesteads. Their astonishment at seeing a white woman strolling past was comical! Finally we arrived at the river. 'There are many crocodiles and hippos in these waters,' remarked Pastor Mizwa nonchalantly, as we sat on the bank. 'Then how do you baptize people in it?' I asked in wonder, as I instinctively tucked my feet up further. 'Quickly,' was his succinct reply.

On our return, men and women emerged from the forest with gifts of freshly picked oranges, and palm and cola nuts, carefully wrapped in emerald-coloured vine leaves. Arriving back at the village, more people pressed little presents into my hands as I walked along – a small bunch of bananas, two fresh eggs, a cob of corn and peanuts. 'I have never encountered such hospitality from strangers in the UK,' I thought to myself.

Suddenly, one of the volunteers ran towards us, pointing to a nearby home. 'There's a sick child in that hut. Please come,' he urged, breathlessly. We hurried after him and found a little girl of about nine sitting on a bed of reeds. Her eyes were enormous in her gaunt face, and her fragile body was thin and emaciated. A worn-looking woman welcomed us in a distracted manner. 'I don't know what to do,' she said in despair. 'My daughter, Christine, has been sick for weeks. She vomits up everything I give her. Now she cannot speak, she is so weak.' I looked at Pastor Mizwa, who remained silent for a while. 'Life is hard here,' he sighed, looking at the little girl compassionately. 'There's no hospital for over seventy kilometres and no transport. If someone is sick, they have to be carried the seventy kilometres to Bonga Yasa in a sling or wheelbarrow. In any case, most people don't have money for hospital fees or medicines.' We prayed over the little girl and, as the Land Rover had been returned to Bonga Yasa, arranged for a volunteer to carry her to the hospital on the back of a bicycle. 'We'll come back and see you later,' I promised, giving Christine a gentle hug.

We spent the rest of the afternoon visiting families, before returning, tired and hungry, to Pastor Mizwa's house. Just as we sat down, one of the volunteers arrived to bring us some sickening news. 'Christine is dead,' he announced. I looked at him with disbelief, feeling stunned and angry. Angry that Christine died for want of accessible medical care. Angry that she died because she was born into poverty. 'It's like this all the time,' said Paul, quietly.

Returning to Christine's home, we found neighbours bearing her little body on a straw mat to the shade of a nearby tree. Women wailed over her, and her mother followed, looking confused and abstracted. Sinking to the ground, she swayed silently from side to side, turning her head this way and that as though looking for something. Kneeling beside her, I held her in my arms. Pastor Mizwa prayed. Paul read some Scriptures, and then asked me to make a speech. Sick to death of words and speeches, I silently continued to hold Christine's mother, as she laid her head on my shoulder.

We spent the rest of the week encouraging PCM's volunteers and the local people, and planning the next steps of our partnership with the PCM team. Hope was birthed during that visit, as PCM and BCT joined hands with each other and with the Pukusu community, to dream dreams and make them happen.

Two years later, Keeley Hayward, BCT's new Training and Project Development Coordinator, would return to Pukusu and discover a place transformed! Where previously there had been wilderness, an ambitious agricultural project had been started. Volunteers had worked together to create fields sown with maize and beans, and other fields were being planned. A huge fishpond, two metres deep, had been created, ready to populate with tilapia fish; twenty-five terraces had been dug above the fishpond for vegetable gardens, and a large area of land had been cleared where the children would be taught to grow spinach, chilli peppers, aubergines and other vegetables. A hut had been built ready for a rabbit-breeding project, and there were plans afoot to teach villagers health promotion and the principles of good nutrition. Community relationships were transformed, as people worked together with a common aim, and the well-being of the children was greatly improved through the love and practical support. Many had come to know Jesus Christ, and an elated Pastor Mizwa told Keeley, 'I praise God because I am seeing the vision God gave me becoming a reality here in Pukusu!'

'You see things as they are and ask "why?" But I dream of things that never were, and ask, "Why not?"'

I was reminded of the quotation by George Bernard Shaw: 'You see things as they are and ask "why?" But I dream of things that never were, and ask, "Why not?"' As a man of extraordinary faith, Pastor Mizwa viewed challenges as opportunities.

I was soon to discover that Pastor Ngolo shared the same spiritual DNA! He was the leader of EPED, and the one whose compelling email and description of his work among street children in the capital city had inspired me to consider coming to the DRC in the first place. So, from Pukusu, I retraced my steps back to Kinshasa to meet this extraordinary man.

12. An odious crime

After the peace and beauty of Pukusu, Kinshasa was like a violent assault on the senses. Chaotic, crowded and crumbling, the city demanded that I remained vigilant and on the alert. As I was driven from the domestic airport to Pastor Ngolo's house, we passed streets with open sewers, piled high with heaps of rotting rubbish. Fetid pools of stagnant water attracted mosquitoes and disease. Thick exhaust fumes added to the noxious smell, exacerbated by the intense, tropical heat. 'Twelve people were shot dead over there last week,' the driver remarked casually, pointing to a busy sidewalk. 'Rebel factions got hot under the collar, and some members of the public got in the way.'

Kinshasa gives the impression of a city in a state of decomposition, flaking and rusting away. There is little by way of beauty. Despite incongruous billboards advertising computers and satellite phones, the roads are seriously eroded, and most buildings are in varying states of decay or disrepair. We passed gated compounds where fabulously rich businessmen live in extravagant opulence, and fragile shacks built on sewers down by the river, populated by the poor.

Pastor Ngolo and his lovely wife Adèle had organized a vibrant reception in the small courtyard of their home, attended by many of the pastors, staff and volunteers working with EPED. Their warm welcome was a veritable antidote to the hostile reception earlier from the police and immigration officials at the airport. A tall, well-built man with an intelligent face and keen eyes, Pastor Ngolo cut an imposing figure. Leaning back in his chair, he shared with me how he had started EPED seven years previously.

'I was a statistician,' he said, 'but I felt called to the ministry and started a theology course. On the way to the college, I would see street children literally sleeping in the streets. Their suffering broke my heart. I couldn't get the picture of them out of my mind. I would stop and speak with them. Finally, when I got to the end of my degree, I decided to make the subject of my dissertation "The Biblical Response to Street Children", but I didn't just want it written on paper. I wanted it to become a living reality. I called together other pastors, and shared with them a vision of starting a work with street children, that had the gospel right at its heart. God moved the hearts of several of the pastors who are now on EPED's management committee. We started visiting the children on the streets, befriending them, and preaching in churches about the need to care for them. EPED grew out of that. We've had little training, and now we've reached the point where we feel we need help in order to grow and expand what we're doing. That was why I wrote to you.'

Listening to his story, I marvelled at the way God had broken the heart of this giant of a man, as he had encountered the plight of street children. There had been no tokenism in his response, no tossing of the odd coin into an outstretched hand to salve his conscience, or empty promises to pray for street children, no leaving it to someone else. Like Pastor Mizwa, he was giving of himself sacrificially and 'shouting the gospel with his life'. His was a truly incarnational ministry. Once again, I had the feeling that I had more to learn from him than he had from me.

In the ensuing days, I accompanied Chico, Leticia, Pastor Lebi and Pascaline, some of EPED's valiant volunteers, into squalid Kinshasa streets and alleyways, heaving market-places and desolate wastelands, to meet with some of the tribes of outcast street children who exist in their thousands in this city. Life on the streets is harsh, and gaining the trust of the children is a slow and difficult process. Resourceful, resilient, and often loyal and generous, the children none-theless become hardened by the daily abuse and hardships. Patiently and lovingly, EPED was helping dozens of children to get off the streets, reconciling them with guardians or family members, where appropriate, or finding adoptive families in the churches. We sat in hovels and houses, shacks and shelters, counselling and praying with families who had children who were HIV-positive. Wherever we went, I was moved and impressed by the passion and commitment of the team who, with humour and compassion, joy and humility, were befriending those whom society despised. Despite their own poverty, some had literally adopted into their hearts and homes those children who had been thrown on to the streets.

There were countless, heart-warming stories of trans-formation. In the ugliness of Kinshasa, stalwart faith and acts of loving-kindness were pushing back the darkness and bringing beauty, life and light. These authentic Christians illustrated what C. S. Lewis meant in *Mere Christianity*:

> When Christians say the Christ-life is in them, they do not mean simply something mental or moral. When they speak of being 'in Christ' or of Christ being 'in them' this is not simply a way of saying they are thinking about Christ or copying Him. They mean that Christ is actually operating through them; that the whole mass of Christians are the physical organism through which Christ acts – we are His fingers and muscles, the cells of His body.[1]

The faith of these people was no cerebral exercise composed of vacuous rituals and empty 'religion', but a flesh-and-blood manifestation of 'Christ in them', born out of the living relationship they experienced with him on a daily basis.

Over the following year, BCT began to partner with EPED and, through our input, enabled the team to scale up their work and give better and more effective care. Forty more churches in Kinshasa were mobilized to link with EPED to reach out to vulnerable children, and, with boldness and courage, the EPED team continued to challenge the government to uphold the rights of children and invest in their care and protection.

However, it was an email from Pastor Ngolo in April 2008 that was to confront BCT with an issue that we had never heard of or encountered before – one that shocked me to the core.

'Dear Madame Susie,' wrote Pastor Ngolo in his usual manner. 'I am writing to tell you about an odious crime that has come to light. Five months ago, an eleven-year-old boy called Aristote and three of his friends, Ruth, Auguy and Lydia, were falsely accused of "witchcraft" by a local pastor and his wife. The latter lit a bonfire and held them over the flames by their hands and feet as an act of exorcism, ignoring their cries for mercy. They then imprisoned them in the church, where they cleaned their wounds with methylated spirit and gave them only enough water, manioc and peanuts to keep them alive. After five months, Aristote escaped. When we heard of his case, we took him to hospital where he is being treated for severe contractures caused by his burns, dehydration and malnutrition. We don't know what state the other children are in. EPED is investigating this case with *Association Africaine des Droits de l'Homme* (AADH), a local human rights organization. Please would you pray and advocate for these children with us?' He had attached a photo of a grossly emaciated little boy with sad, luminous eyes, and the flesh burnt from his groin, legs and stomach. Sickened and stunned, Keeley and I wept together.

But gradually, tears turned to anger. John Templeton, the businessman and philosopher, once wrote, 'If we were holier people, we would have been angrier, oftener.' In the face of such cruelty and injustice, it was impossible to remain dispassionate. In all of my experience, I had never before come across anything quite so horrific. It wasn't just that children were being brutally abused. Atrocities were being carried out by those who professed to be followers of Christ, doing these terrible things in his name. On investigation, we discovered that across different parts of Africa, Asia, Latin America, and even in Europe and the UK, tens of thousands of children are being accused of 'witchcraft'. Some are subjected to 'deliverance rites' that involve varying degrees of abuse. Others are thrown out on to the streets. According to a 2006 Human Rights Watch Report, an estimated 30,000 children live on the streets of Kinshasa, DRC. Of these, an estimated 70% were accused of 'sorcery' in their homes before coming to the streets.[2]

In the DRC and in many other regions of the world, sickness, death and misfortune may be interpreted through the lens of a worldview where two spheres co-exist – the invisible realm of the occult, spirits, witches and mystic forces, and the visible world. Economic, social and political upheaval, poverty, conflict and sudden changes in marital, family and societal relationships may create conditions where fear and suspicions flourish and harmful beliefs and practices take root, as people try to make sense of adversity and the complex world around them.

It was in just such an environment that Aristote and his friends had been tortured, by those who used their power and influence to further their own ends.

The more we delved into the issue, the more we knew we had to do something about it. But what? By then, Brenda

Hunt had joined BCT as our Office Manager and Catherine Dellbridge was our new Administrator. Both are women of feisty faith and huge compassion. Brenda, Catherine, Claire, Keeley and I began to pray daily for Aristote's healing, for the rescue and release of Lydia, Ruth and Auguy, and for justice to be done. Our prayer partners interceded with us, as we fed them news updates, and EPED and AADH campaigned tirelessly on behalf of the children. After three months, those who had perpetrated the abuse were arrested and imprisoned, although the 'prophetess' escaped and fled to another province. It was discovered that twenty-one other children had been held captive at the church with Aristote and his friends. Those holding them got wind that the church was to be raided by the police, and, by the time the latter got there, all the children had been ordered by their captors to 'run away'. Only three of these children were subsequently traced. EPED never did find out what happened to Aristote's friends, in spite of searching for them for months.

The day after my birthday, on 12 November 2008, I settled on the sofa with Jeremy for some television. Perhaps there was a movie worth watching? Instead, we found ourselves viewing a Channel 4 *Dispatches* documentary called *Saving Africa's Witch Children*. It was very far from relaxing. Featuring the work of Stepping Stones Nigeria (SSN), it showed footage of children in the Niger Delta region of Nigeria being accused of 'witchcraft' and abused by so-called 'bishops' and 'pastors', who were being paid relatively large sums of money to carry out the harmful 'deliverance' rites. Gary Foxcroft, SSN's Director, was featured with Sam Itauma, leader of the Child Rights and Rehabilitation Network (CRARN), courageously confronting the perpetrators and rescuing children who had been brutally treated. I was sickened but encouraged at the same time. Here was an agency prepared to confront the issue and do something about it! Contacting Gary, I arranged to meet up with him. A warm, down-to-earth character, he spoke candidly of his frustrations. As a secular organization, SSN was having difficulty getting churches and their leaders in the UK and other parts of the world to confront and engage with the issue. 'What can BCT do to help?' he asked.

I personally shared his frustration with the lack of action. Having discussed the issue with various Christian groups and individuals in previous months, I had received the same response over and over again: 'This is evil stuff. Don't get involved. It's too risky. You don't know what you'll be letting yourself in for.'

Our default response in the UK seemed to be a desire to keep safe, to stay within our 'cappuccino-coffee' comfort zones and talk a good fight.

I couldn't believe my ears! Where were the champions for these children? Pastor Ngolo and others like him were at the coalface, stopping at nothing for the sake of the children, while our default response in the UK seemed to be a desire to keep safe, to stay within our 'cappuccino-coffee' comfort zones and talk a good fight. The theologian Karl Barth once said that 'Comfort is one of the siren calls of our age'. In his book *The Eye of the Needle*, Roy McCloughry wrote, 'We need to recover our courage and our belief in the adequacy of God if we are to be risk-takers and people of faith.'[3]

Small though we were as an organization, we knew that this 'child-witch' issue was something that God was calling BCT to respond to, and that, with his leading, we could do so with confidence. There was no 'no-go' zone with him, so there wouldn't be with us either. We had heard the cry of Aristote and his friends, and with God's help we would act.

13. 'The trumpet has been blown!'

Threading my way through the busy market place of Mombele, I arrive at the tall, red metal gates of EPED's refuge for girls. The heat of the day is oppressive, and it's a relief when the gates swing open and I can enter and sit in the shade of the veranda. A pleasant, airy, bungalow-style house is surrounded by tall, grey walls, topped by vicious-looking shards of metal, designed to put off intruders. The gates are locked, and a guard is on duty at all times, in order to protect the girls who have come to find sanctuary here.

As I flop into a plastic chair, Pascaline, Coordinator of the centre, brings me some water. It's February 2010. Keeley is in Pukusu, visiting Pukusu Children's Ministries, while I stay behind in Kinshasa to follow up on those attending an important, one-day 'round-table' meeting. The aim is to bring together lawyers, church leaders, and representatives from street children's networks, governmental departments and human rights agencies in Kinshasa, to encourage them to work collaboratively to combat the 'child-witch' phenomenon.

The idea for the 'round table' had come to me while praying, a couple of weeks before Keeley and I were due to depart from the UK for the DRC. It had taken hard work on

EPED's behalf to organize it at such short notice, but it had been a huge success. The year before, the DRC government had ratified a Child Protection Code in which it had been made a criminal offence to accuse a child of witchcraft, let alone abuse them. Much of our 'round-table' discussions had therefore centred on what needed to be done to ensure that the government and society as a whole actively upheld this law. By the end of the day, a new network had been birthed called 'Réseau des Intervenants pour la Lutte contre les Phénomènes Enfants dits Sorciers' (RILPES), (The Network for Those Fighting the Phenomenon of So-called 'Child Witches').[1]

There's the sound of suppressed whispers and giggles, and, as I chat with Pascaline on the refuge veranda, some young girls sidle up and start playing with my hair. They've started to be at ease with me over the past few days. They chatter and laugh while pointing out my freckles to one another and creating plaits and ponytails out of my locks! Nearly all of them are here because family members have accused them of 'witchcraft' and thrown them out on to the streets. One lays her head on my lap. They are hungry for affection, and yet constantly quarrel and fight. It's no wonder they have behavioural problems. The abuse they have suffered has left them scarred inwardly and outwardly. Twelve-year-old Belinda[2] is restless and disruptive. When her aunty died, her mother accused Belinda of killing her through 'sorcery'. She was hauled to a church, where the pastor confirmed that Belinda was indeed 'guilty' of cursing her aunt. Her mother took her home, where her uncle held her down and ran a burning hot iron over her back and legs in an attempt to 'burn out the demons', while her mother looked on. Belinda fled and spent the next two years on the streets, before being discovered by EPED.

As ten-year-old Christianne[3] patiently tries to teach me a song, she seems like any 'normal' girl. But when her parents divorced, her father accused her of witchcraft. Christianne strongly denied this, so her father took her to the river and threw her in. Miraculously, she didn't drown, but was swept six kilometres downstream before she managed to reach the riverbank and climb to safety. After eighteen months of living on the streets, she was rescued by EPED, and was now on the slow road to recovery. Most of the girls in the refuge are being treated for sexually transmitted diseases at a local hospital, due to the rape and sexual abuse they have endured on the streets. It's hard even to imagine what they have been through.

It was girls like Belinda and Christianne who caused BCT to start our 10:10 Campaign. This ongoing campaign is a call for people everywhere to pray, advocate and act to bring an end to the abuse and suffering of children branded as 'witches'. As I had prayed about the campaign, the name had come to me from John 10:10, where Jesus says, 'The thief's purpose is to steal and kill and destroy. My purpose is to give them a rich and satisfying life' (NLT). The lives and childhoods of these children are being robbed, but Christ wants to bring them life in all its fullness.

Much of my time, and that of the BCT team, began to be spent raising awareness of the issue, writing materials and updates, and mobilizing agencies and individuals to get involved. As a result, hundreds of people in the UK and around the world became aware of the issue and started to pray.[4]

A couple of days after my visit to the girls' refuge, Pastor Ngolo and I hire a car to make the journey to Mama Rose, a 'revivalist' pastor who has taken in nine children accused of being 'witches'. As we drive past the disintegrating heap that was once President Mobutu's palace, a rabid police officer thrusts his face into the driver's window, demanding to know who we are and where we are going. He shouts and waves his arms around, working himself into paroxysms of anger, then orders us to turn back for no reason whatsoever. It's obvious that he wants a bribe, and equally obvious that this is an excellent time to pray, which I do, while Pastor Ngolo calmly gets out of the car to reason with him.

The EPED team face this kind of treatment on a daily basis, and do so with grace, courage and a refusal to give in to corruption. Suddenly the policeman calms down and waves us through. We heave a sigh of relief, and the rest of the journey passes without incident. On our right runs River Congo, with Brazzaville on the opposite bank. Fishing pirogues ply its waters, and men standing waist-deep cast huge nets, a scene that has remained unchanged for centuries.

Finally, we arrive in a small town on the outskirts of Kinshasa. As we come to a stop, a petite woman, neatly dressed in a multicoloured traditional robe and matching head wrap, steps up to greet us. 'You are welcome,' says Mama Rose, before leading us off down a narrow, undulating path. After following a small stream, we enter a lovely village where I see beauty for the first time in two weeks, free from the terrible pollution that taints Kinshasa. Even the air is clear. We arrive at the whitewashed home of Mama Rose, who seats us in the cool shade of a grassy bank.

In the DRC, it is predominantly so-called 'revivalist' pastors who instigate or confirm allegations of witchcraft. The majority have never been to theological college, and possess no training in ministry and very little Bible knowledge. In this country there are no regulatory procedures, and anyone can set up as a church leader. All that is needed is a place in which to meet and a loud voice. Many conmen and women falsely parade as 'church leaders', knowing that they can make money from vulnerable 'followers'. Accusing children of witchcraft and carrying out 'deliverance rites' is a profitable business, and many of these unscrupulous leaders demand big money. Others may be genuine in their motivation, but, because of poverty, have had little or no access to training, leading to ignorance and malpractice. Still others may have had training, but belong to denominations where there is little accountability or oversight, making it easy to fall into errant beliefs and practices. Many subscribe to a syncretism of Christian and 'traditional' or 'reinvented' cultural beliefs, and fervently believe that they are doing society a service by 'delivering' children from 'evil spirits'.

Unusually, Mama Rose is a 'revivalist' pastor who, through the influence of EPED, has changed her attitudes and practices. When parents brought their children to Mama Rose for 'deliverance', she would take them and pray for them to be delivered from 'demons', never questioning what was behind the parents' accusations. In this country, as in other areas where this phenomenon is prevalent, any child perceived as being 'different' is at risk of being accused of witchcraft by family and community members. This can be a child with disability, or one who is exceptionally bright, or even one who wets the bed.

Changing deeply-entrenched attitudes and beliefs takes time, but Pastor Lebi, an EPED volunteer, has been patiently teaching and influencing Mama Rose to change her understanding and practice. 'Because of Pastor Lebi's example and teaching, I no longer believe these children are "witches",' she explains, as she sits with us outside her home and shares her story. 'I now want to care for those who have been mistreated.' She goes on to explain that she has taken in nine children, all of whom have been accused of witchcraft. They live with her and her own seven children. 'I love them like my own children, and God provides for us,' she says, as she deftly pours us water from small plastic bags. Going to a window of her home, she calls, and a group of children of all ages come spilling out. Mama Rose looks at them with pride. 'When they first arrived, they were sick and thin, but just look at them now.' The children all look strong, healthy and undeniably happy and well adjusted. According to Mama Rose, some of them had been abandoned on the streets and cruelly treated before coming to her. In time, they may be reunited with family members, if appropriate, but, in the meantime, they share a new family.

One by one, the children come and shake hands with us, and then start to play, pulling out a big box of broken toys from under a battered table. 'Would you like to have tea with our dolls?' asks one little girl. I readily accept her invitation, and she pours me an imaginary cup of tea that I pretend to drink.

Mama Rose now teaches her church about child protection. She attended the round-table meeting held the week before. As we say farewell to her, she gives us an enormous bag of fresh greens from her garden as a parting gift. 'I want to influence others to care for these children now,' she says, as she walks us back to the stream, 'and to lead by example.'

The next week is packed with visits to agencies and individuals who attended the round table. By the end of the week, we've formed good relationships with the members of RILPES, and shared plans for concerted action. I criss-cross Kinshasa on buses that are no more than decrepit old vans, inside which are rough, freestanding benches that slide up and down and from side to side, as the vans hurtle along. Every time we hit a rut, which is often, we fly forwards or backwards, depending on the momentum. It's a cosy way of getting to know fellow-travellers, as I frequently land in their laps or collapse on the back of the person in front of me.

On one memorable occasion, the entire side of the bus in which we are journeying falls off, much to everyone's amusement, and the alarm of the man on whom it lands. The grace, patience and fortitude of the average Congolese man or woman is phenomenal. They have an innate sense of style and humour, and an ability to make the best of their circumstances that is truly admirable. As always, it's in environments such as those that prevail in Kinshasa that I have met the real heroes of the planet: men and women, such as those involved in EPED, Pukusu and RILPES, who overcome adversity with courage, selflessness and an indomitable spirit.

Pastor Ngolo had introduced me to Reverend Dr André Bokundoa, General Secretary of the Communauté Baptiste du Fleuve Congo (CBFC), one of the largest and oldest Baptist streams in the DRC. 'Let's pay Reverend Bokundoa another visit,' I suggest, as Pastor Ngolo and I sit outside with his family one evening, in the relative cool of their yard, playing the time-honoured game of swatting mosquitoes.

Two days later, we arrive in Reverend Bokundoa's air-conditioned office, sweating and dishevelled from yet another arduous journey. An affable, portly man in a brightly patterned shirt, Reverend Bokundoa welcomes us warmly. Having lived in the UK, he speaks fluent English. I get straight to the point: 'What is the CBFC doing to act and advocate on behalf of the multiple thousands of children in the DRC who are abandoned and tortured for being so-called "witches"?' Reverend Bokundoa silently considers the question a moment, his eyes searching his desk. Looking up, he ruefully replies, 'We are doing nothing.'

We spend the next hour listening to his thoughts and outlining key child-protection issues. At the end of our meeting he says, 'You have come into my room like a bomb. My eyes have been opened. How have we missed this? Why have we not been involved in protecting and caring for these children? What could have been more important than this?' He stands up. 'We must act immediately. I want you to pass this fire on to the governing leaders of the CBFC at their meeting on Thursday evening. I will arrange it.'

Reverend Bokundoa is as good as his word, and, on the Thursday evening, I find myself addressing the Reverend Anderson Mundeke, Regional Secretary of the CBFC for

Kinshasa, and seven other leaders. Reverend Bokundoa has also come in person to lead the meeting. By the end, it has been agreed that a new child-protection structure will be established in the CBFC, and a meeting will take place in the next couple of weeks to draw up a strategic action plan. 'We will work as one,' says Reverend Bokundoa. 'Enough of words! I want to see action.'

Walking out of the door after the meeting, Pastor Ngolo turns and winks at me. 'We got what we came for,' he says, smiling. 'The trumpet has been blown!'

Since then, through the 10:10 Campaign, BCT has begun to 'blow the trumpet' in churches in the UK as well, training them in childcare and protection. As I write, BCT and SGM Lifewords (as they are now called) are planning to work together with EPED to pilot the Pavement Project programme among street children and those accused of 'witchcraft' in Kinshasa, to help restore broken identities and self-worth. Plans are being made to run trauma-training workshops for agencies that are part of RILPES, as a means of enabling them to bring healing to children like Belinda and Christianne.

During our latest visit to the DRC, Keeley and I met a pastor who is working with EPED to bring restoration to children at risk. On our return, he wrote:

> Praise God, your presence in the DRC helped me to understand once again that we are not alone, but are part of the army of God to make manifest his reign of justice, peace and goodwill by the power of the Holy Spirit. God's reign is never passive. He manifests himself through love in action shown by his people towards others, as we defend and take the part of the weak and marginalized in society.

'That's it!' I thought. 'Perhaps that's what it means to be a "resistance fighter", as we refuse apathy, or to accept the way things are in this world, but choose instead, in humility and God's strength, to make manifest his reign of love, justice, peace and goodwill, defending and taking the part of the weak and marginalized, resisting evil and overcoming evil with good. By this definition, I reflected, all of us who are Christ's followers are called to be "resistance fighters" within the sphere of influence that he has given us.'

Postscript: 'Disturb us, Lord'

BCT recently celebrated its tenth anniversary with an event that brought together individuals who have played an invaluable part in helping us to transform the lives of countless children during the past decade. We looked back over all that had been achieved, and shared inspirational stories from VINODI and Wukwashi Wa Nzambi, a wonderful project we are partnering with in Zambia, helping children with disability. At the end of a great evening, Karen Brickley, BCT's Chairperson and a woman of great faith and vision, chose to close with a prayer attributed to Sir Francis Drake:

Disturb us, Lord,
When we are too well pleased with ourselves,
When our dreams have come true
Because we have dreamed too little,
When we arrived safely
Because we sailed too close to the shore.

Disturb us, Lord, when
With the abundance of things we possess
We have lost our thirst

For the waters of life;
Having fallen in love with life,
We have ceased to dream of eternity
And in our efforts to build a new earth,
We have allowed our vision
Of the new Heaven to dim.

Disturb us, Lord, to dare more boldly,
To venture on wilder seas
Where storms will show Your mastery;
Where losing sight of land,
We shall find the stars.

We ask you to push back
The horizons of our hopes;
And to push us into the future
In strength, courage, hope, and love.

This we ask in the name of our Captain,
Who is Jesus Christ.[1]

My heart leapt as I heard these words, resonating as they do with my own heartfelt prayer and desires, not only for the worldwide Christian church, but also for The Bethany Children's Trust and for the lives of Jeremy and me. 'Never let us cease to dream of eternity, Lord, or to allow our vision of the new heaven here on earth to dim!'

For the past couple of years, Jem has been a full-time leader at our church in Putney. The word that Bob, our former pastor, heard as he prayed all those years ago has now become a reality. We don't know what lies ahead, but neither of us wants to 'settle' or to begin to 'sail too close to the shore'. We simply want to 'dare more boldly', to make every day of our lives count 'for our Captain, who is Jesus Christ', and to be ready to go wherever he leads.

Since I finished writing this book, tragic news came through from DRC. In October 2010, people from a neighbouring village came to attack the people of Pukusu, following the death of a head teacher. Typically, Pastor Mizwa (pictured overleaf) courageously placed himself between the two groups and begged them not to fight. The mob hacked, beat and burned him. He later died from the injuries he had sustained, at the age of seventy-four. He died, as he had lived, a spiritual giant who did not count the cost, but sacrificed everything he had for the love of God and his fellow men. Pukusu had been robbed of one of its finest.

As I look back over my life, I'm amazed at the journey that God has taken me on, and at all that has been made possible. Mine has been a story that tells of his love and faithfulness and extraordinary grace. I ask myself, 'Did it start all those years ago on the floor of that hut in Chisumbanje, as I held that dying woman in my arms and heard those words, "No Susie, the question is, what are *you* going to do about it? " Or did it start long before then, when, as a young child, a little girl dreamed of being a resistance fighter?' The truth is, I believe it was birthed in the heart of God before time began, and the story will never end.

'Pukusu had been robbed of one of its finest.' Pastor Mizwa and his wife

Notes

3. A 'Nightingale Nurse'
1. Name changed to protect identity.
2. Name changed to protect identity.

4. 'We've never come across a disease like this before'
1. Name changed to protect identity.
2. Name changed to protect identity.
3. Name changed to protect identity.

5. 'You are a resistance fighter'
1. Statistics sourced from www.avert org/hiv-aids-history.htm.

7. Miracles of transformation
1. Shona words for 'aunties and grandfathers'.

9. Holding up the arms
1. Crucially, the Pavement Project programme continues to initiate the process of healing in the lives of countless street children around the world, and to affect the way Christian workers counsel and communicate with them.

10. Breaking the silence

1. David Anns was BCT's Administrator, Tom Green became Communications Coordinator, and Gill Grant was BCT's Project Support and Development Coordinator. Gill was Director of The Bethany Project in Zimbabwe from November 1999, and returned to the UK in 2002.

12. An odious crime

1. C. S. Lewis, *Mere Christianity* (Macmillan, 1952).
2. 'What Future? Street Children in the Democratic Republic of Congo', April 2006, *Human Rights Watch*, Vol. 18, No. 2(A).
3. Roy McCloughry, *The Eye of the Needle* (IVP, 1990).

13. 'The trumpet has been blown'

1. RILPES is now energetically acting and advocating to prevent witchcraft accusations and to rescue and seek justice for children being abused in this way.
2. Name changed to protect identity.
3. Name changed to protect identity.
4. BCT has been able to link with those individuals and agencies that want to take further practical action.

Postscript: 'Disturb us, Lord'

1. Prayer of Sir Francis Drake, 1577, before departing from Portsmouth to circumnavigate the globe.

The Bethany Children's Trust
putting children first

To find out how you can get involved in the work of
The Bethany Children's Trust through prayer,
advocacy, giving and practical action, visit
BCT's website: www.bethanychildrenstrust.org.uk
email: admin@bethanychildrenstrust.org.uk
Tel: +44 (0)20 8977 7571
The Bethany Children's Trust – Registered Charity 1073817